AF575305

PICASSO

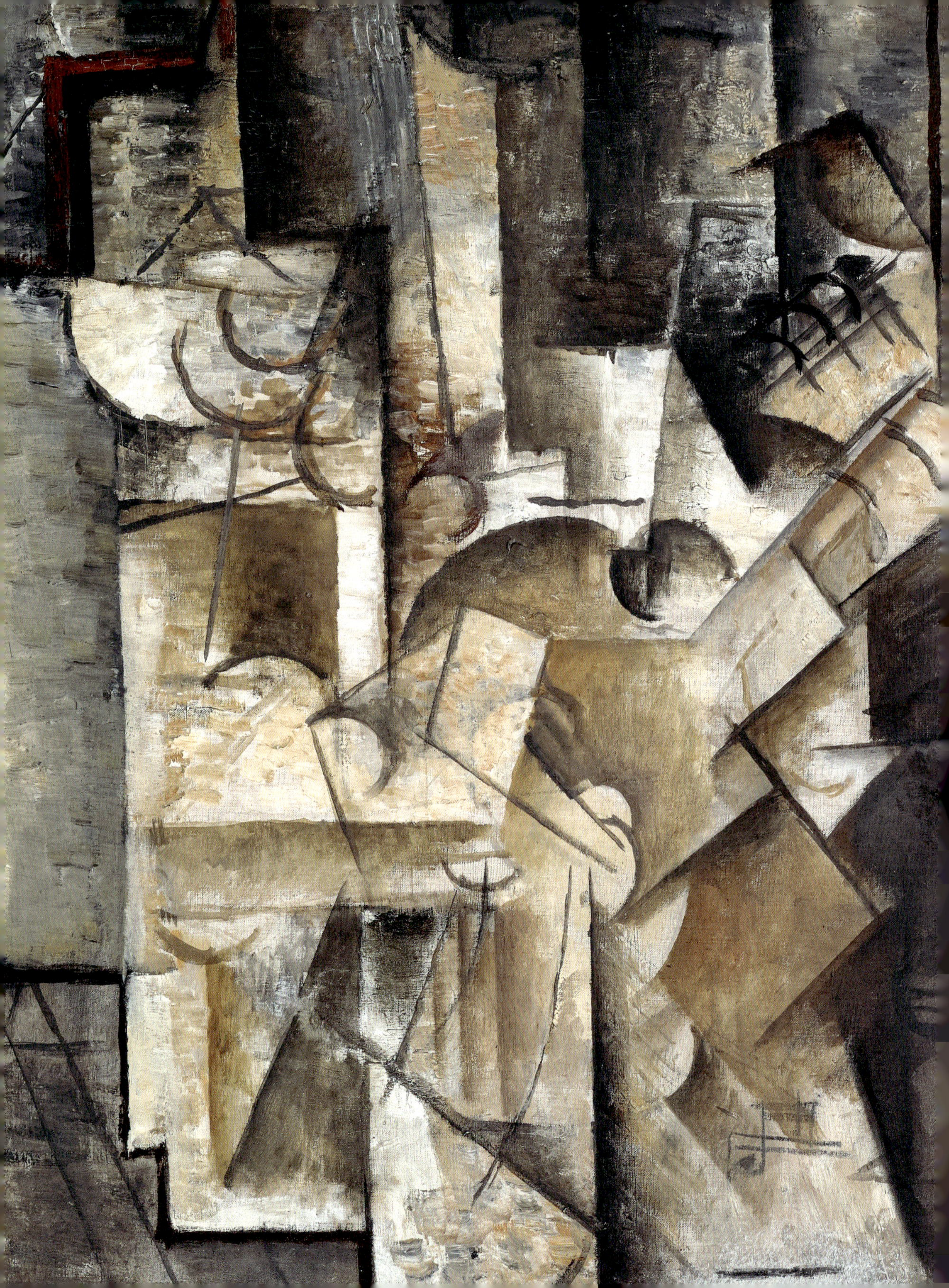

LEONARD A. LAUDER
RESEARCH CENTER FOR MODERN ART

PICASSO

A CUBIST COMMISSION IN BROOKLYN

ANNA JOZEFACKA
WITH LAUREN ROSATI

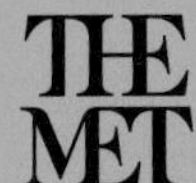

THE METROPOLITAN MUSEUM OF ART, NEW YORK
Distributed by Yale University Press, New Haven and London

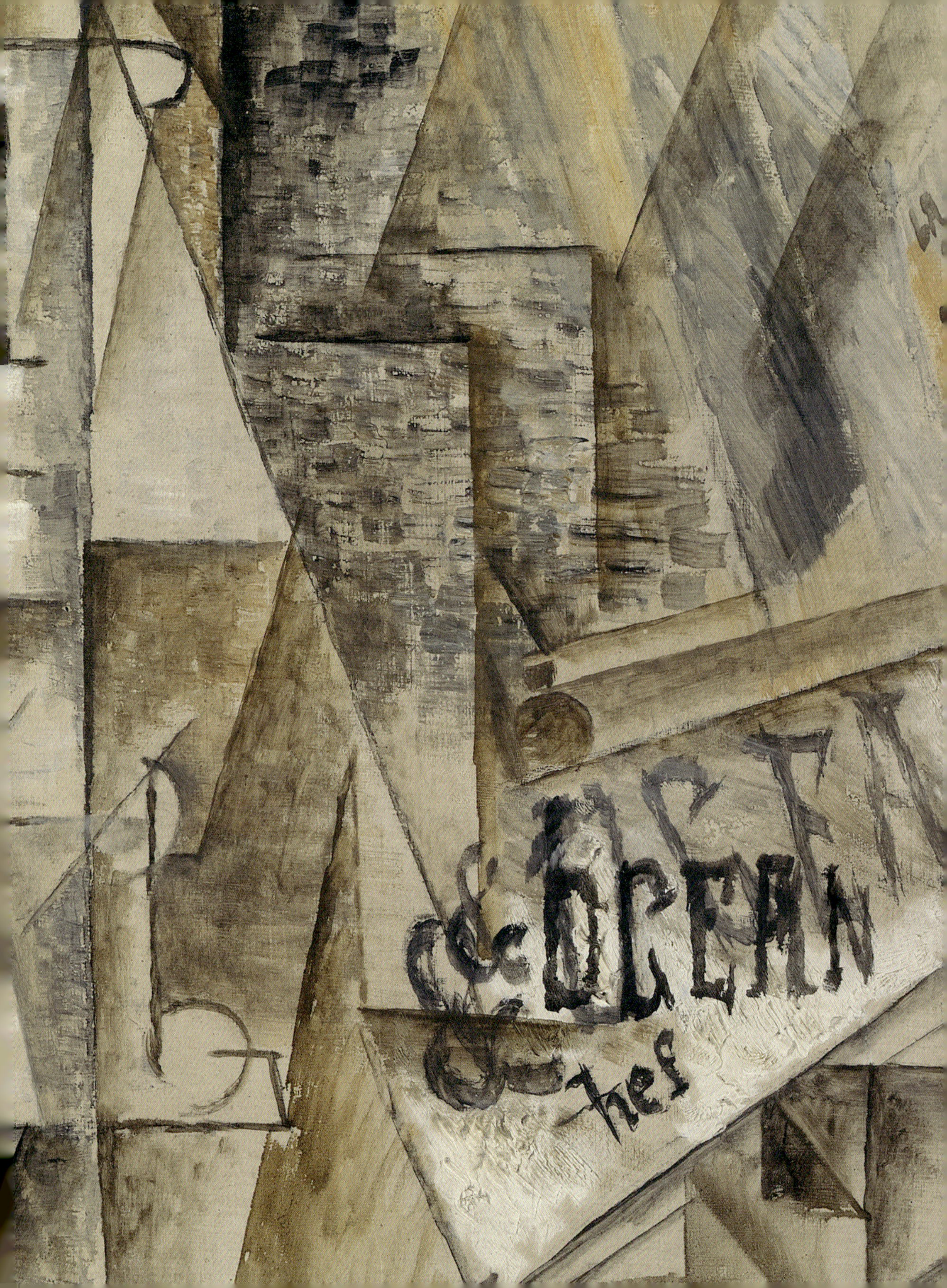
OCEAN
hef

CONTENTS

FOREWORD

In recalling his first impression of Pablo Picasso, Hamilton Easter Field wrote in a 1921 column in his hometown newspaper the *Brooklyn Daily Eagle*, "He looked like a genius just as Walt Whitman looks like a genius. You could not remain unmoved in his presence." Deeply stirred by Picasso's work, Field commissioned a suite of eleven decorative panels in 1909 for the library of his ancestral home in Brooklyn Heights, the oldest residential section of the borough. Picasso accepted the challenge and worked on the panels for several years, a project that was never completed. This important, albeit little-known chapter of Picasso's radical Cubist idiom, is the focus of this revelatory exhibition—the first ever on the subject. Presented by The Metropolitan Museum of Art under the auspices of the Leonard A. Lauder Research Center for Modern Art, *Picasso: A Cubist Commission in Brooklyn* brings together a group of extant panels with related works and archival documents, affording us a fresh angle on Cubism and Picasso's transcendent work.

I congratulate the Research Center, The Met's vibrant hub for scholarship on modern art, now in its tenth year of existence. This project powerfully conveys its commitment to innovative research that expands our understanding of modern art in general and Cubism in particular. *Picasso: A Cubist Commission in Brooklyn*, the second exhibition organized by the Research Center, was conceived and curated by an alumna of its prestigious fellowship program. Anna Jozefacka, now an independent scholar, held a Leonard A. Lauder Postdoctoral Fellowship in Modern Art from 2015 to 2017, during which time she studied the relationship between Cubism and interior architectural space. The present exhibition and accompanying publication, which were realized with the assistance of Lauren Rosati, Associate Curator in the Department of Modern and Contemporary Art, and Research Projects Manager in the Leonard A. Lauder Research Center for Modern Art, represent the culmination of that work. I would also like to acknowledge the essential roles of Stephanie D'Alessandro, the former Curator in Charge of the Research Center and now the Leonard A. Lauder Curator of Modern Art and Senior Research Coordinator in the Department of Modern and Contemporary Art, and Neil Cox, the current Head of the Research Center, for bringing it to fruition.

The exhibition represents The Met's contribution to the international Picasso Celebration 1973–2023, which honors the fiftieth anniversary of the artist's death. It also marks the first exhibition devoted to the artist's oeuvre at The Met since the comprehensive survey of its Picasso holdings in 2010. Since then, the Museum's inventory of the artist's work has been transformed by the promised gift of Leonard A. Lauder's outstanding Cubist collection. Centered on the art of Picasso, Georges Braque, Juan Gris, and Fernand Léger, the phenomenal gift comprises (as of this writing) eighty-nine paintings, sculptures, and works on paper, thirty-six of which are by Picasso alone. Like the previous exhibition mounted by the Research Center, *Birds of a Feather: Joseph Cornell's Homage to Juan Gris* (2018), the current project draws inspiration from works in the collection, in this case, two drawings by Picasso, *Standing Female Nude* (1910) and *Standing Woman* (1912).

This exhibition also introduces to Met audiences the figure of Hamilton Easter Field, who has strong ties to the Museum. In 1909, prior to his departure for Europe and his fateful meeting with Picasso, Field loaned a group of works to The Met from his own collection. As reported by *Brooklyn Life* on October 16, 1909, the Museum's visitors admired a "large nude by [Paul-Albert] Besnard, an angel by [Francesco] Botticini . . . other paintings which were long attributed to Botticelli, and a fine Greek marble torso of the Third Century before Christ." In subsequent years, Field continued to contribute to The Met's exhibitions, including the *Loan Exhibition of Impressionist and Post-Impressionist Paintings* (1921), which was the Museum's first presentation of works by Picasso. As an art critic for the *Brooklyn Daily Eagle*, Field never missed an opportunity to cover the Museum's latest offerings, be it a survey of Gustave Courbet's paintings or Egyptian antiquities. Today, dozens of works formerly in Field's collection, including Japanese prints and French drawings, are in our holdings. We are thrilled to be able to unite a series of Picasso paintings initially intended for Field's home, and in doing so, bring to light a little-known chapter in Cubism's history.

We owe a tremendous debt of gratitude to Leonard A. Lauder for his extraordinary vision and philanthropy, and to the other invaluable and anonymous supporters of the Research Center for their own dedication to the study of modern art. Through their generosity, the Leonard A. Lauder Research Center for Modern Art makes this exhibition and publication possible. Lastly, I would like to acknowledge the outstanding cooperation of institutional and private lenders. Their full commitment to this project cannot be overstated.

Max Hollein
Marina Kellen French Director and CEO
The Metropolitan Museum of Art

ACKNOWLEDGMENTS

Any project regarding Pablo Picasso and his Cubist idiom leans on legions of scholars who have dedicated their careers to assessing this challenging body of work from one of the most important and prolific Western artists. Their contributions have informed our research and compelled us to bring the story of Hamilton Easter Field's commission to the fore.

The generosity of public and private lenders ensured the realization of this undertaking, and we owe our gratitude to Cécile Debray, Director, Cécile Godefroy, Head of the Centre d'Etudes Picasso, Emilia Philippot, former Head of Collections, Marie Liard-Dexet, Collections Registrar, Joanne Snrech, Paintings Conservator, and Laurent Le Bon, former Director, at the Musée National Picasso-Paris; Kaywin Feldman, Director, Harry Cooper, Senior Curator of Modern Art, and Jay Kruger, Head of Painting Conservation, at the National Gallery of Art, Washington, D.C.; Gabriel Montua, Head of the Museum Berggruen, Staatliche Museen zu Berlin, and Udo Kittelmann, former Director; Christiane Lange, Director, Staatsgalerie Stuttgart; Matthew Teitelbaum, Ann and Graham Gund Director and CEO, Edward Saywell, Chair, and Benjamin Weiss, Leonard A. Lauder Senior Curator of Visual Culture, Department of Prints and Drawings, at the Museum of Fine Arts, Boston; Valerie Paley, Senior Vice President and Sue Ann Weinberg Director of the Patricia D. Klingenstein Library, and Marilyn Satin Kushner, Curator and Head, Department of Prints, Photographs, and Architectural Collections, at New-York Historical Society; Pauline Vidal, Research Manager, Emilie Faust, Conservator, and Tiphaine Besnard, Archivist and Photo Library Manager, at Fundación Almine y Bernard Ruiz-Picasso para el Arte, Madrid; Maite Blanco, Registrar, at Museo Picasso Málaga; the late Robert Stonehill and his wife, Helene; the Laurent family; and three private lenders. We recognize the goodwill and special interest afforded to this project by Olivier Berggruen, Bernard Ruiz-Picasso, and José Lebrero Stals, Artistic Director, at Museo Picasso Málaga. We extend our thanks also to the Picasso Administration, and to Christine Pinault in particular for her assistance and support of this project.

A number of institutions assisted us in our research, among them the Archives of American Art, Smithsonian Institution, Washington, D.C.; Beinecke Rare Book and Manuscript Library, Yale University, New Haven, Connecticut; Brooklyn Museum; Brooklyn Public Library, Center for Brooklyn History; Columbia University Libraries,

New York; Grolier Club, New York; Institut National d'Histoire de l'Art, Paris; Kunsthaus Zürich; Musée des Arts Decoratifs, Paris; Musée d'Orsay, Paris; New-York Historical Society; New York Municipal Archives; New York Public Library; Picasso Archives, Musée National Picasso-Paris; Rensselaer Libraries, Rensselaer Polytechnic Institute, Troy, New York; and Thomas J. Watson Library at The Metropolitan Museum of Art, New York.

This exhibition and publication are a testament to The Met's steadfast leadership and dedicated staff. We are grateful for the support of Max Hollein, Marina Kellen French Director and CEO. Stephanie D'Alessandro, the former Curator in Charge of the Leonard A. Lauder Research Center for Modern Art and now the Leonard A. Lauder Curator of Modern Art and Senior Research Coordinator in the Department of Modern and Contemporary Art, has been an unstinting advocate for this project since its inception in 2018; her critical assistance and expertise have enabled the success of this project. We thank Neil Cox for his encouragement and careful attention to this project since his appointment as Head of the Leonard A. Lauder Research Center for Modern Art in 2021, as well as the members of the Research Center's Advisory Committee. We also would like to express our thanks to Laura James, Associate Administrator, for her expert support. In the Department of Modern and Contemporary Art, we owe our gratitude to David Breslin, Leonard A. Lauder Curator in Charge, and his predecessor Sheena Wagstaff, former Leonard A. Lauder Chair, and Katy Uravitch, Senior Manager for Administration, Operations, and Collection Management, as well as her predecessor, Pari Stave. Sean O'Hanlan, former Research Associate, graciously stepped in to lend her assistance in spring 2022, for which we are particularly grateful. We also thank Mary Chan, Collections Manager, and Cynthia Iavarone, Senior Collections Manager, and the Department's technicians, Lionel Carre, Zachary Hewitt, Brooks Shaver, and Nalani Williams.

Colleagues from the Exhibitions Office, in particular Quincy Houghton, Deputy Director of Exhibitions, Zoe Tippl, Senior Exhibitions Project Manager, and Marci King, Associate Exhibitions Project Manager, expertly managed the details of this project, and Allison Barone, Associate Registrar, deftly coordinated and oversaw all important logistics. Rebecca Noonan Murray, Senior Associate General Counsel, helped us with provenance inquiries, Emily Balter, Assistant General Counsel, Amy Lamberti, Associate General Counsel, and Meryl Cohen, Chief Registrar, oversaw our indemnity and immunity applications, and Elizabeth Kornhauser, Alice Pratt Brown Curator of American Paintings and Sculpture, The American Wing, provided crucial assistance during the initial stages of our research.

Pivotal to this project was the input of The Met's extraordinary conservators, Isabelle Duvernois, Paintings Conservator, Daniel Hausdorf, Objects Conservator, and Rachel Mustalish, Sherman Fairchild Conservator in Charge of the Department of Paper Conservation. Every visit to their labs resulted in new revelations.

We cherished every meeting with Daniel Kershaw, Exhibition Design Manager, and June Yoon, Graphic Designer. Their resourcefulness, perseverance, and design acumen helped us to achieve our vision. Thanks also to Chelsea Garunay, Exhibition Design Manager.

We had the great privilege to work with The Met's outstanding Publications and Editorial team led by Mark Polizzotti, Publisher and Editor in Chief, and including Michael Sittenfeld, Associate Publisher for Editorial, Peter Antony, Associate Publisher for Production, Christina Grillo, Production Manager, and Elizabeth De Mase, Senior Image Acquisitions Manager. We couldn't have asked for a better editor and catalogue designer than Kayla Elam and Roy Brooks, respectively.

Along its long and winding road, the project benefited from the advice, support, encouragement, and critical input of many individuals, among them Emily Braun, Doreen Bolger, Elizabeth Cowling, Julia May Boddewyn, Harold Dean, Andrew Dolkart, Susan H. Edwards, Sheri Farber, Michael FitzGerald, John H. Field, Lindsay Ganter, Pepe Karmel, Joan Kay, Lynda Klich, Marge Laurent, Holly Laurent, Luise Mahler, Alice Momm, Robert Parker, Malka Simon, Laurie Stein, Anna Tome, Vérane Tasseau, and Doug Wayne.

We owe thanks to the Leonard A. Lauder Research Center for Modern Art as a whole, not only for fostering this project's development, but also for its financial support of the exhibition and its publication.

Our deepest gratitude is reserved for Leonard A. Lauder, whose boundless passion for modern art and its histories provided the original impetus for this project.

Anna Jozefacka and Lauren Rosati

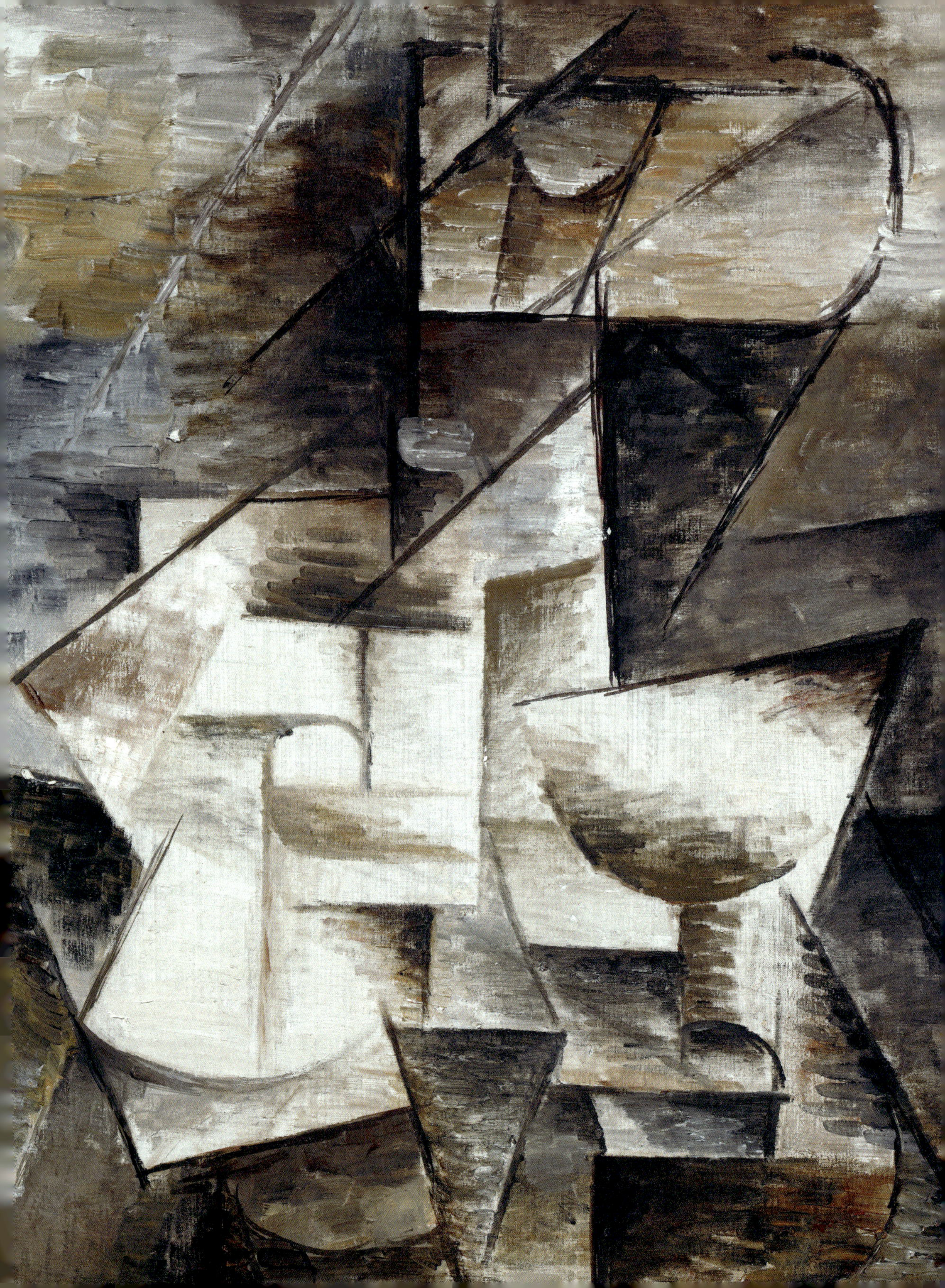

PICASSO: A CUBIST COMMISSION IN BROOKLYN

ANNA JOZEFACKA

In 1910 Pablo Picasso embarked on a novel venture: a decorative commission for the Brooklyn home of artist, collector, and critic Hamilton Easter Field. The two men had met in Paris through a mutual friend, likely in fall 1909. By August the following year, Picasso received Field's formal request for up to eleven paintings, including three overdoor panels, to adorn the walls of his library. If carried out as envisioned by Field, the commission would have challenged the artist to move beyond easel painting and create an ensemble of individual Cubist pictures conceived as an enveloping aesthetic whole. The date of the commission coincided with a critical moment in the development of Picasso's Cubism. While spending the summer of 1910 in the Spanish seaside village of Cadaqués, Picasso brought his painting to the brink of abstraction. How he would adapt this style of painting, with its monochromatic palette and barely recognizable content, to a decorative program with various mural formats—some unusually large and others unusually narrow—was among many challenges facing the artist. Although Picasso keenly engaged with these new considerations, at the time of Field's death from pneumonia in 1922 at the age of forty-nine, the commission was still incomplete.

The story of the paintings and the relationship between the two men went unrecognized for decades, owing to Field's initial desire for confidentiality and Picasso's lifelong discretion about his artistic practice. Determined to establish his legacy but at the same time reluctant to divulge studio secrets, Picasso left behind just one piece of written evidence about the commission in his vast personal archive, which, following his own death in 1973, required years to sort and catalogue. As the art historians Judith Cousins and Hélène Seckel (later Hélène Seckel-Klein) were searching through the archive in the 1980s, they came across the letter Field sent to Picasso on July 12, 1910, containing a description of the library, floor plan, elevation, and dimensions of the individual wall areas to be covered (for a reproduction and translation of the letter, see pp. 89–91).[1] Following Cousins and Seckel's discovery, William Rubin, then the director emeritus of the Department of Painting and Sculpture at the Museum of Modern Art, New York, began to reassess the unusual sizes and proportions of some of Picasso's Cubist paintings beginning with *Nude Woman*, a 1910 canvas with an imposing height of six feet but a width of barely two feet (pl. 1).[2] As Rubin wrote in 1989, "It was while musing on why Picasso would have chosen such a constraining format that it suddenly occurred to me that he might not have chosen it at all, but have had it imposed on him."[3]

Applying the criteria of corresponding or near-corresponding measurements provided by Field in his 1910 letter, Rubin tentatively attributed *Nude Woman* and eight other works to the Field commission. He considered extant paintings as well as one known only from a period photograph of the artist's studio. Focusing on the commission's unfulfilled status, Rubin speculated that Picasso had soured on the project because he had realized that Cubism was not suited for a traditional decorative ensemble. Moreover, the artist was likely unable to maintain continuity across the varied sizes of the assigned wall areas, one measuring as large as 72 ⅞ by 118 ⅛ inches (185 by 300 centimeters). As Rubin conjectured, "the fragmented style of Picasso's early Cubism, fashioned primarily for single-figure 'iconic' pictures, did not lend itself to extension over large canvas."[4] In 1996 John Richardson, the artist's biographer, brought to light new research, including two additional period photographs, that enlarged the number of paintings potentially linked to the Field commission.[5] These findings also upheld Rubin's conclusion that Picasso's Cubism was not well-suited for a large-scale, multipart project.

With only these two accounts of the Field commission as starting points, *Picasso: A Cubist Commission in Brooklyn* deepens the inquiry into this unique episode within Picasso's Cubist period by considering more closely how the artist engaged with the project. The proposed room, encompassing narrow vertical and horizontal as well as mural-size spatial areas, certainly offered Picasso the opportunity to explore the possibilities and limitations of his developing approach to the pictorial representation of bodies and objects. The space's distinct architectural configuration also presented him with a new vantage point from which to consider his Cubist compositions. Significantly, Picasso had to weigh considerations for the various wall spaces from his studio in France, rather than on-site. From this angle, Picasso followed an established precedent of easel painters who fulfilled similar assignments by working within the confines of their studios. Many decorative commissions, or *décorations*, no longer occupy the wall areas for which they were commissioned (or, like this project, were never installed in the first place), yet the vestiges of their intended architectural sites remain. Indeed, some of the completed Field panels were eventually released by Picasso, and today all extant works function as independent easel paintings, gracing the walls of private rooms and public galleries. This book accompanies an exhibition that brings together for the first time six paintings associated with the project, allowing for unprecedented opportunity to experience these large and unusually proportioned canvases in the same room. The text that follows presents new research on Field, Picasso, and the proposed installation site, and situates the project within the rich European decorative painting tradition, offering thus far unconsidered points of reference for Picasso's Cubism.

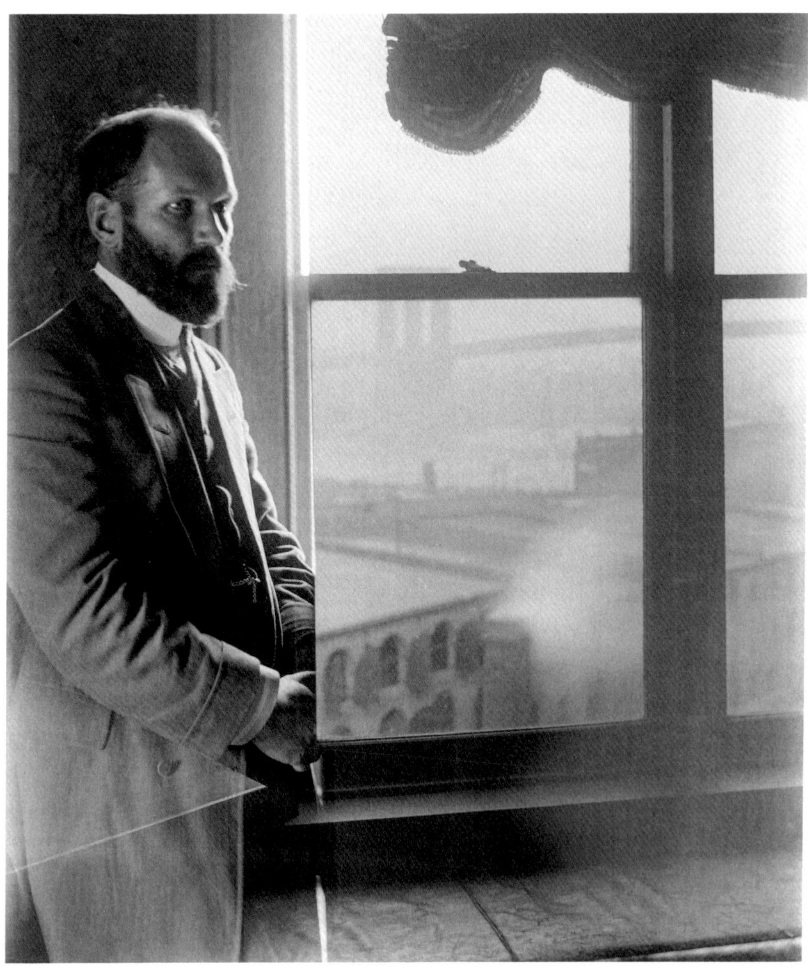

Fig. 1
Paul Haviland, *Hamilton Easter Field in his Brooklyn home at 106 Columbia Heights*, 1905–15. Print from glass negative, 10 × 8 in. (25.3 × 20.2 cm). Musée d'Orsay, Paris, Fonds Paul Burty Haviland, Don Nicole Maritch-Haviland et Jack Haviland, 1993 (PHO 1993 2 64)

THE ARTIST AND HIS PATRON

Born in Brooklyn in 1873 to a prominent local Quaker family, American painter Hamilton Easter Field trained in Paris in the last decade of the nineteenth century (fig. 1).[6] Although he permanently returned to Brooklyn in 1902, he continued to regularly travel to Europe. On two occasions, from 1905 to 1906 and 1909 to 1910, he remained there for more than a year. It was sometime during the latter sojourn that he met with Picasso and offered him the commission. Although Field's precise whereabouts during the trip have not been established thus far, it is known that he left for Europe in February

1909, spent a portion of the summer in Florence and a period of time from November 1909 to May 1910 in Rome, and that on his return journey he crossed Europe, passing through Zurich, Paris, and London.[7] Significantly, a mid-October 1909 report from *Brooklyn Life*—a weekly review of art, literature, and the social engagements of the Brooklyn elite—suggests that he might have resided in Paris prior to settling in Rome for the winter.[8] If this was the case, his encounter with Picasso and his work may have taken place then, at Picasso's new apartment (and studio) on the boulevard de Clichy.[9]

Frank Burty Haviland, Field's French American cousin and a friend of Picasso, likely carried out the introduction, perhaps during one of Picasso's short-lived "at home" hours held on Sundays (fig. 2). Field had become acquainted with Burty Haviland and his older brother, Paul, during his art student years in Paris. The relationship continued once Field returned to Brooklyn: from 1902 to 1915, Paul was working for the family porcelain business in New York, where Frank joined him from 1907 to 1908.[10] In addition to family ties, and despite their age differences (Paul was seven and Frank thirteen years younger than Field, respectively), the three bonded over a mutual passion for the arts. Grandsons of important French art critic Philippe Burty, Paul developed a keen interest in photography, while Frank (who adopted his grandfather's last name) took up painting. In one of his photographs, Paul captured Field in his Brooklyn home posing with the Brooklyn Bridge in the distance (see fig. 1).

Field recalled his first impressions of Picasso in a 1921 exhibition review of Frank's paintings at Brummer Gallery in New York. Remarking on Picasso's artistic hold on his cousin, Field noted his own enchantment with the Spaniard: "Naturally I met the new god and fell under his influence quite as much as [Frank] Burty [Haviland] had. It would be difficult for an artist not to feel the charm of Picasso, whose eyes alone suggest a full, rich, emotional and intellectual nature."[11] When he first met Picasso, Field was also likely accompanied by his French-born protégé, eventual heir, and associate in his wide-ranging art-related ventures, Robert Laurent, who took painting lessons with Frank for a time in Paris before turning his attention to sculpture.[12] The degree of Field's familiarity with Picasso's output before he made his commission offer is unclear. If their initial encounter took place in the fall of 1909, the American would have seen, among others, Picasso's latest paintings in his studio. Made during the summer in the Catalan village of Horta de Ebro (present-day Horta de Sant Joan), Spain, these figures, landscapes, and still lifes featured legible but antinaturalistic forms that became characteristic of Picasso's early Cubism. By that year, Frank Burty Haviland had likely also begun to acquire several works by the artist, including examples from his earlier Rose Period style. Although Field would have been made

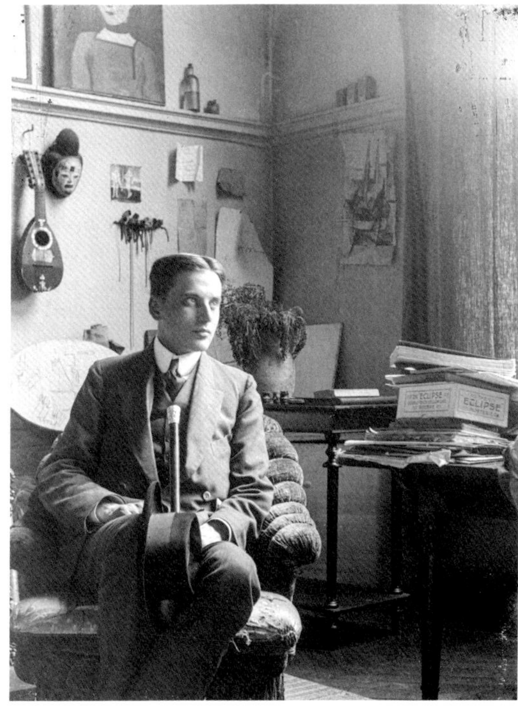

Fig. 2
Frank Burty Haviland at Pablo Picasso's boulevard de Clichy studio, Paris, ca. 1911–12. Picasso Archives, Musée National Picasso-Paris

aware of Picasso's rapidly evolving work based on his experience in the artist's studio and his probable encounters with Burty Haviland's Picasso collection, neither patron nor artist could have foreseen the radical dissolution of subject and form that would occur within a year.

Throughout his career, Picasso balanced artistic freedom with an enterprising approach to selling his work. Branching out into private decorative commissions would have allowed him to gain greater independence from art dealers. In his decision to take the commission, Picasso could have been also excited by the fact that Field was not just any client but a fellow artist who respected the creative process. There is no archival evidence to suggest that Picasso involved either of his dealers—Daniel-Henry Kahnweiler or Ambroise Vollard—in his interactions with Field. At this time the artist had no formal contract with either one. Indeed, John Richardson speculates that the project might not have materialized had Kahnweiler been involved in the negotiations: "Since he had more to lose than gain, Kahnweiler is likely to have discouraged Picasso from devoting so much time to an unprofitable venture."[13] On the other hand, a pragmatic dealer may well have insisted on a contract that, at a minimum, stipulated a deposit, payment installments, and a delivery schedule for the paintings. The lack of such concrete arrangements may account for why the commission, seemingly based on a gentleman's verbal agreement, never came to fruition.

Even so, any payment Field offered surely played a role in Picasso's decision. During fall 1909 and spring 1910, the artist was temporarily short on cash but embracing a more sumptuous lifestyle.[14] In September 1909 he moved out of the ramshackle quarters of the Bateau-Lavoir in the heart of Montmartre to a larger and more comfortable bourgeois apartment at 11 boulevard de Clichy within the same Parisian neighborhood. That month, Picasso held a private viewing in the new studio of his 1909 Horta del Ebro paintings to raise funds for his expenses.[15] Notably, Kahnweiler bought little at this time from the artist, and Leo Stein, Gertrude's brother and previously an enthusiastic patron, neither approved of, nor sought to buy, Picasso's newer, Cubist works. Assuming that Field was indeed in Paris that fall, it is conceivable that Burty Haviland brought his artist cousin to his Spanish friend as a potential client.

Although Field indicated in his 1910 letter to Picasso that he shared the news of their arrangement privately with some of his friends, who in turn were "keenly interested" in seeing his "decorations," he was initially close-lipped about the commission and his interactions with the artist. It was only a decade later, in his *Brooklyn Daily Eagle* newspaper columns, which appeared during regular art seasons from March 1919 until his death in April 1922, that Field intermittently published recollections of his conversations about art with Picasso and indicated how the commission came about during their meeting in 1909.

He first revealed these details in a column dating from late November 1919. In this text, Field shared with his readers the two interests he had developed while an art student in Paris some twenty-five years earlier.[16] First, he had discovered the old master Renaissance painters Tintoretto and El Greco, who engaged with what Field called "deformation" and "abstraction" to produce antinaturalistic effects in their work. He recognized Picasso as both a successor to El Greco (a comment that was bound to please the Spaniard, who admired the painter) and an innovator who took the Renaissance artist's affinity for antinaturalism further than any prior painter.[17] In Field's assessment, Picasso's art progressed from "emotion through deformation" in, presumably, the Blue and Rose Periods, to the "almost pure abstraction" of, again presumably, Cubism.[18]

Second, Field wrote that while abroad he had come to recognize the power of *décoration*—a reference to murals or paintings of nonstandard size created for specific architectural spaces and made directly upon the wall or set flush with the wall and delineated by a framing device. As Field emphasized, his parallel interests in antinaturalism and *décoration* came together in 1909 when he met Picasso. Though taken with the Spaniard's art, Field told Picasso then and there that he had "made a mistake in merely painting easel pictures, for abstract art needed an entire room or better a house in which all furniture should be subordinated to the decorations which would cover the flat walls. He should get orders to decorate buildings. I could not offer him a house to decorate, but I had a library with no pieces of furniture except the bookshelves and a few low chairs."[19]

Though decorative ensembles may seem old-fashioned and antithetical to the interest of modernist artists and their commitment to the inherent autonomy of line, form, and color, many of Picasso's contemporaries had engaged with such large-scale, multipart works. Field and Picasso might have shared opinions on the many nineteenth-century mural paintings found in Parisian churches and public buildings. In the same November 1919 column, Field confided that as an art student he had formed a preference for Paul-Albert Besnard over Pierre Puvis de Chavannes, two important and successful French painters of large public commissions. He recalled spending more time at the city's Ecole de Pharmacie (School of Pharmacy), for which Besnard had executed a series of mural paintings (1883–88), than at the Panthéon showcase of Puvis's work (1874–79).[20] Field's observations might have triggered Picasso to disclose, to the contrary, his esteem for Puvis as evidenced in the dreamy mood and palette of his Blue Period work. Indeed, during his early stays in Paris, Picasso visited the Panthéon to sketch from Puvis's mural cycle paintings depicting the life of Saint Genevieve.[21]

In other *Brooklyn Daily Eagle* columns, Field relayed that he and Picasso also discussed the French artist Camille Corot, a mutual favorite, as well as academic art. Field recalled, "When I used to talk with Picasso about painting there was one name which always aroused his enthusiasm: Corot. He seemed to enjoy above all else in Nineteenth Century art the early work of Corot. I have much of the same taste as the founder of the cubist school although I do not show it in my own painting."[22] This conversation might have been prompted by the exhibition of Corot's figure paintings on view at the 1909 Salon d'Automne (a selection that made a deep impression on Picasso).[23] In March 1922, just a month before his death, Field quoted Picasso on the work of academically trained painters: "'It is beautiful because it is so clear. The houses are houses and the walls have the quality of walls. Each thing is just what it is supposed to be and I can tell you it took much feeling at the start to abstract from each object its fundamental quality. That this form of painting has degenerated into mere reiteration of a banal formula does not take from the splendor of the original conception.'"[24]

In 1966 Robert Laurent stated that he remembered "Picasso being so excited [about Field's project], saying that it was just the sort of commission he had been hoping for."[25] While Laurent's account ought to be taken with a grain of salt, as it came more than half a century after the fact, there is no reason to doubt Picasso's enthusiastic reaction. The commission had much to offer the artistically ambitious Spaniard. And the timing was right. As a regular visitor to Paris salons during this period,[26] Picasso would have registered the ongoing popularity of decorative commissions—in both academic and modernist styles—for residences of private patrons.[27] Fellow painters Maurice Denis, Henri Matisse, and Pierre Bonnard had all been engaged by the Russian industrialists Ivan Morozov and Sergei Shchukin, who had also shown an interest in Picasso's work, although no commissions had come his way. At the 1908 Salon d'Automne, Denis exhibited five mural-size panels of his *Psyche* cycle (1908; State Hermitage Museum, Saint Petersburg), rendered for the stately music salon of Morozov's palace in Moscow.[28]

More importantly, during the same Salon at which Denis exhibited the five *Psyche* panels, Matisse unveiled the even more radical *Harmony in Red (The Red Room)* (1908; State Hermitage Museum, Saint Petersburg), noted in the catalogue as a "decorative panel for a dining room."[29] It was the first of several works commissioned by the textile magnate Shchukin from Matisse for his Moscow mansion, and was followed by the pendant mural-size paintings *Dance (II)* (fig. 3) and *Music* (1910; State Hermitage Museum, Saint Petersburg), which were presented at the Salon d'Automne of 1910.[30] Picasso would not have missed these two bold and brilliant paintings at the 1910 Salon, where they caused an uproar. At the same time, his first panels for Field were underway in his studio. Indeed, the Picasso scholar Pierre Daix later opined that his burning artistic rivalry with Matisse could have compelled Picasso to accept the American's proposition.[31]

An unrealized decorative commission that Matisse pursued in fall 1909 for a different client enriches the context for the Field project, attesting to the competitiveness not only of Picasso but also of his new patron. That September, while in Paris, the American art historian Bernard Berenson paid a visit to Matisse's studio and asked the artist to paint decorations for the library in his Florentine residence, Villa I Tatti. But, before Matisse had even submitted his proposal, Berenson awarded the commission to René Piot, Matisse's artist friend and another exhibitor of decorative paintings at the 1908 Salon d'Automne, who had been courting the art historian for about a year.[32] Field had known Berenson and his wife, Mary, since 1903, and the three socialized regularly in Europe and the United States.[33] It is likely that Field would have met Berenson in Paris in fall 1909 and, most importantly, known of his intentions for I Tatti. Field also knew Piot, and according to Field, Piot's letter of introduction gained him an entry to the writer André

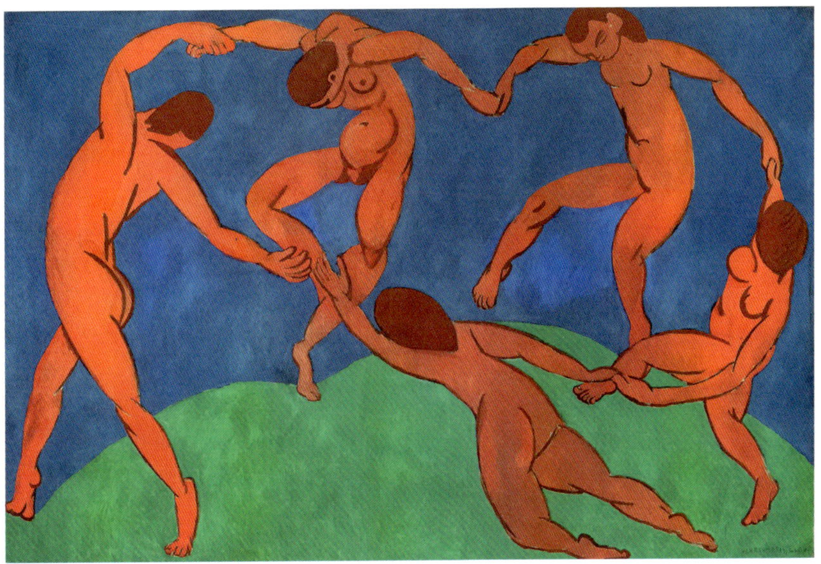

Fig. 3
Henri Matisse, *Dance (II)*, 1909–10. Oil on canvas, 102 ⅜ × 154 in. (260 × 391 cm). State Hermitage Museum, St. Petersburg

Gide's home in Auteuil (Paris) to view the fresco decoration Piot had carried out from 1908 to 1909.[34]

As a fine art painter whose primary medium was easel painting, Picasso would have likely noted that his fellow artists' Salon entries for decorative panels functioned just as well as independent works. The autonomy of a work of art certainly preoccupied avant-garde artists of Picasso's generation. In 1912 Cubists Albert Gleizes and Jean Metzinger wrote: "The picture bears its pretext, the reason for its existence, within it. You may carry a picture with impunity from a church to a drawing-room, from a museum to your study. Essentially independent, necessarily complete, it may need not to immediately satisfy the imagination: on the contrary, it should lead it, little by little, toward the fictitious depths in which the coordinative light resides. It does not harmonize with this or that environment: it harmonizes with things in general, with the universe: it is an organism."[35] In many ways, Denis and Matisse achieved this, putting forth a new modern rendition of decorative painting. However, Denis's and Matisse's approaches to their respective commissions differed—a reflection perhaps of Denis's deep appreciation of the Italian Renaissance fresco tradition and his background as a member of the Nabis, the late nineteenth-century artist group, which had a history of completing decorative painting for private interiors as well as elevating the status of decorative painting above that of easel painting.[36] Unlike Matisse, Denis was careful to fit his cycle into its in situ location (fig. 4). In

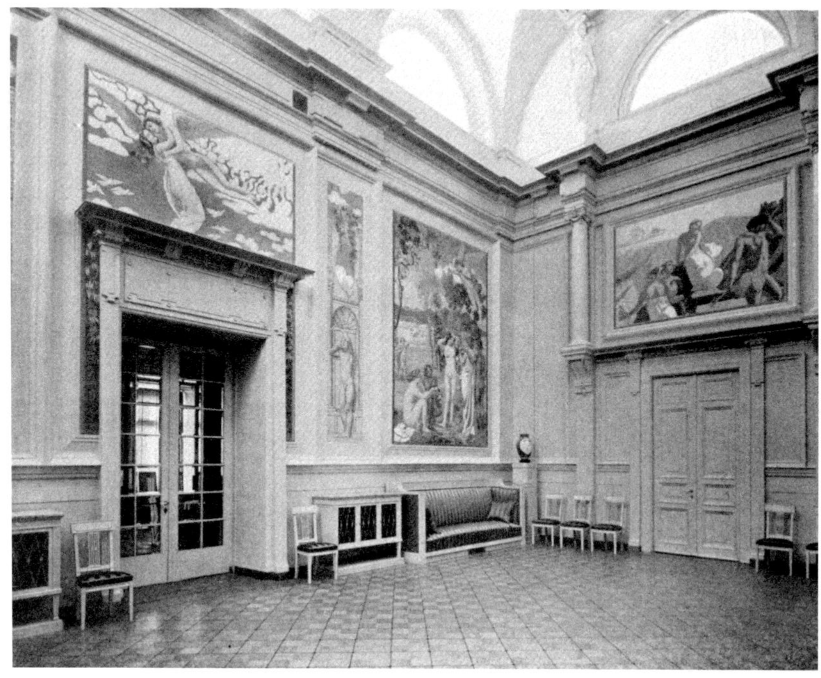

Fig. 4
Installation view of Maurice Denis's panels from the *Psyche* cycle (ca. 1908–9) in Ivan Morozov's music salon, published in *Apollon* magazine (St. Petersburg), 1912

early 1909 he followed his five *Psyche* paintings to Moscow, where he made adjustments to integrate them into the music salon. He not only altered the compositions of the five panels but once back in Paris expanded the *Psyche* cycle by two overdoor and six narrow side panels for a better fit in the room. Considering them of equal importance to his five main panels, Denis exhibited these additional paintings publicly at the end of 1909 in a Paris gallery prior to shipping them to Russia.[37] Matisse's visit to the Shchukin residence in 1911 didn't lead to such results, and instead his paintings retained their autonomy even after they were installed there.[38] The challenge posed by creating paintings for a specific architectural space was a factor for Picasso as well, and his approach more closely aligned with that of Matisse. As Richardson has stated, "in the absence of any decorative experience, Picasso was obliged to do the very thing that Field had counseled him against: conceive the project as a series of easel paintings."[39]

In late May 1910 Field spent several days in Paris before returning to New York.[40] His visit coincided with an exhibition at Wilhelm Uhde's Notre Dame des Champs gallery of Picasso's 1908 to 1910 work, which was assembled from Uhde's and Frank Burty Haviland's collections. Field undoubtedly used the occasion for yet another interaction with Picasso and possibly discussed practical details of the commission, such as the function and decor of the room, the medium of the decorations, time frame of delivery, and crucially, payment.[41] That same month, the American magazine *The Architectural Record* published Gelett Burgess's article "The Wild Men of Paris," the first U.S. report on the art of the Parisian avant-garde.[42] It included the first public appearance of Picasso's groundbreaking *Les Demoiselles d'Avignon* (1907; Museum of Modern Art, New York), which was reproduced in black and white. Notwithstanding the touch of "scandal" surrounding a style of art that was incomprehensible to most, the timing and publicity could not have been better for Field: it affirmed his aesthetic precocity in engaging the foremost "wild man" to decorate his Brooklyn home. The meeting with Field was likely still fresh in Picasso's mind when he wrote to his friend and patron Gertrude Stein on June 14 informing her that he was about to leave Paris for the coastal village of Cadaqués in Spain's Catalan region, and that by next winter he had "to do a decoration for America, for a cousin of Haviland's."[43] (For a reproduction of the letter, see p. 89.)

BIBLIOTHECULA

By the time Picasso wrote to Stein in June, Field had already sailed for New York.[44] Upon returning to Brooklyn after nearly a year and a half abroad, he wasted little time in sending Picasso the information necessary to begin his work. Field's letter, written in French and postmarked in Brooklyn on July 12, was sent to Burty Haviland's Paris address, further attesting to his cousin's role as an intermediary. The letter was then forwarded, eventually reaching Céret, where Burty Haviland was then staying. Picasso received it in Spain by still-unknown means sometime after August 2.[45]

In the letter Field included a detailed description of the room, accompanied by a hand-drawn elevation of one of the walls (fig. 5), a floor plan (fig. 6), and outlines of each wall section allocated to Picasso—all of which are identified by a letter of the alphabet, A through K. These visual aids harken back to Field's initial and short-lived architectural studies, which he pursued at American universities prior to his 1894 move to Paris to train as a painter.[46] In the letter, Field conveyed the long and narrow dimensions of the library (approximately 10 by 23 feet, or 3 by 7 meters) and its features, including a single window, three doors, and electric lighting, as well as a built-in bookcase in place of wainscoting. He also provided the dimensions of each wall, beginning with the door on one of the room's two narrow sides—marked as A on the floor plan and presumably the primary entry

Fig. 5
Detail of the wall elevation
in Field's letter

Fig. 6
Detail of Field's schematic
floor plan of the library

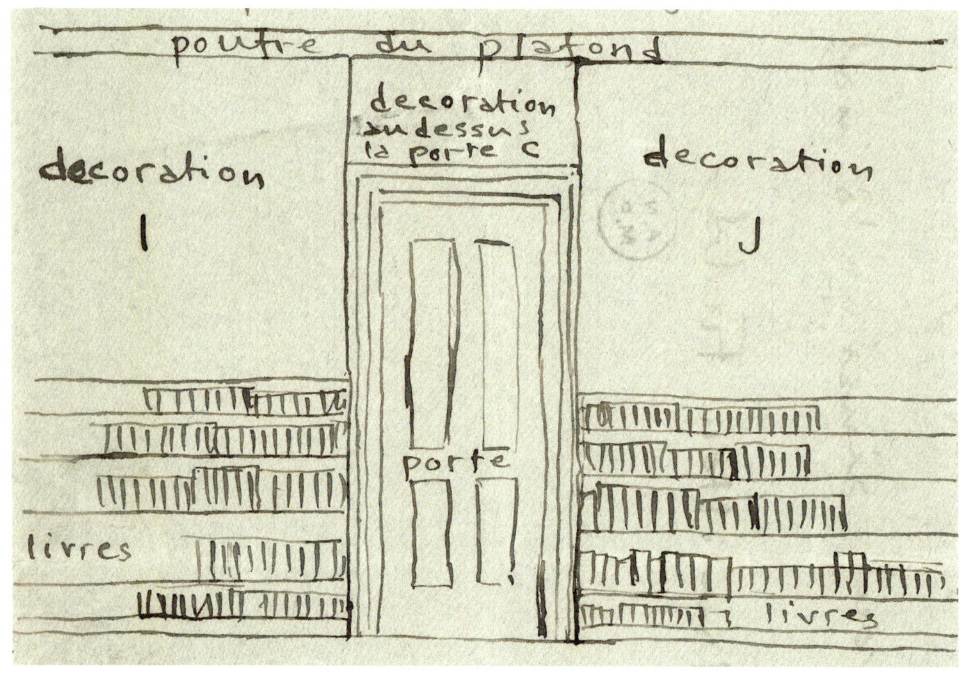

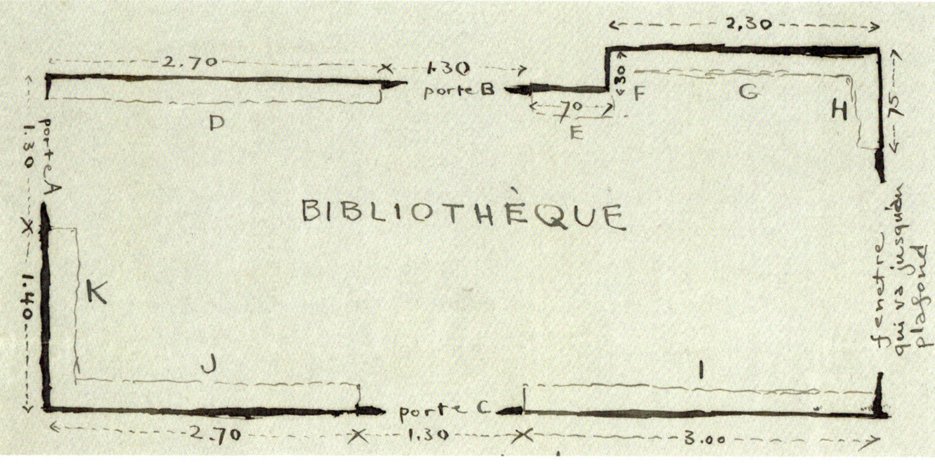

point into the library—and then moving clockwise around the room. There were ten wall spaces in total, not counting the wall area F mentioned in the letter as likely too narrow to receive a decorative panel (a meager 12 inches, or 30 centimeters, wide). The seven wall spaces above the low wraparound bookshelves had uniform heights of 72 ⅞ inches (185 centimeters), but were of varying widths, from 27 ⅝ to 118 ⅛ inches (70 to 300 centimeters). Additionally, there were three overdoor areas of equal dimension: 19 ¾ by 51 ¼ inches (50 by 130 centimeters).

In his schematic drawing Field clearly envisioned Picasso's paintings taking up each wall area in its entirety. Given the room's intimate size, it was clear that each painting would be seen in close proximity and together would provide an immersive experience for the viewer. Crucially, Picasso did not have to accommodate any preexisting decor or period wall fittings, such as decorative wood paneling and plaster crown molding. Instead, he could focus on conforming his paintings to the stipulated wall areas. Field's letter, however detailed and informative, did not convey the room's location within the house. If Picasso was left wanting more from Field's description, Frank Burty Haviland could have supplied further detail: he was familiar with his cousin's home in Brooklyn from his time in New York and could have assured the artist that the library stood on the principal or parlor level of the residence, where it was part of a suite of reception rooms.

Built by James S. Haviland (Field's maternal grandfather), the ancestral home at 106 Columbia Heights stood toward the southern end of Quaker Row, a collection of seven row houses situated on the west, or waterside, of Columbia Heights, a street running between Orange and Cranberry Streets (fig. 7).[47] Acquired and developed by a group of local Quakers (some sharing family ties) in 1845, the block was part of the steady transformation of Brooklyn Heights from rural community to affluent residential urban enclave of the then-independent city of Brooklyn, which was only a short ferry commute to downtown Manhattan. Laid out along the edge of the bluff that gave Brooklyn Heights its name, Columbia Heights was the most prestigious street in the area, affording its residents panoramic views of New York Bay and beyond (fig. 8). The Quaker Row properties encompassed the entire steep slope of the bluff itself, stretching downward as far west as Furman Street at water level, with residential lot sizes more generous than those typical in New York and Brooklyn. The local Brooklyn press habitually described the house at 106 Columbia Heights as a "mansion."[48]

From its Columbia Heights facade, the building stood at three stories, with a high-windowed subbasement and low attic (fig. 9). On the right side of the facade, the asymmetrically placed main staircase led up to the front entrance at the parlor-floor level, elevated above the street. Despite its

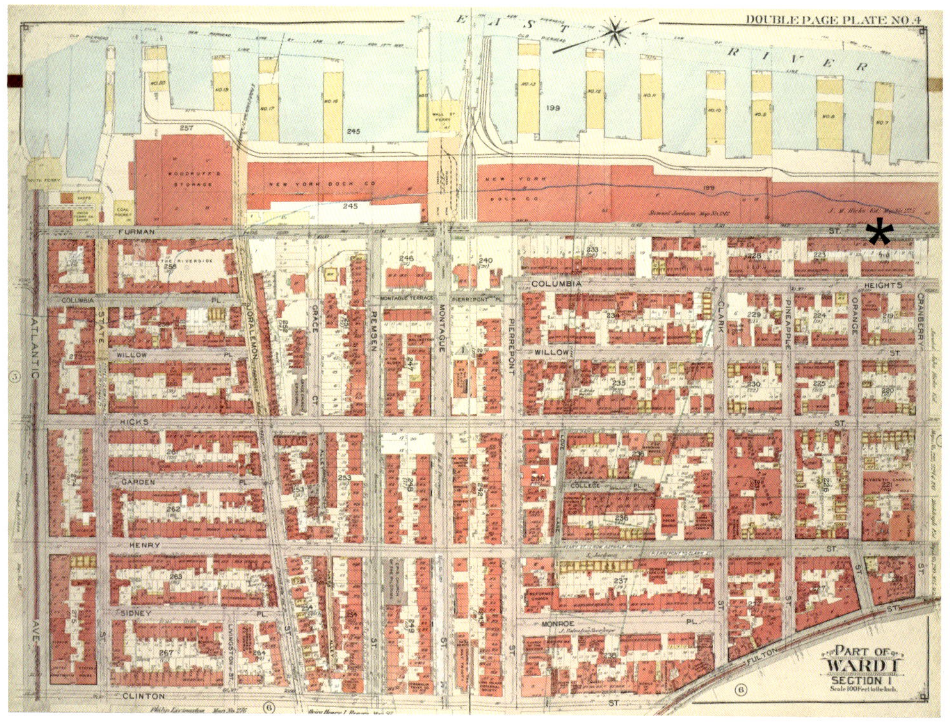
DOUBLE PAGE PLATE NO. 4
EAST RIVER
NEW YORK DOCK CO.
WOODRUFF'S STORAGE
FURMAN ST.
COLUMBIA HEIGHTS
COLUMBIA PL.
MONTAGUE TERRACE
PIERREPONT PL.
WILLOW PL.
WILLOW ST.
HICKS ST.
GARDEN PL.
COLLEGE PL.
HENRY ST.
SIDNEY PL.
MONROE PL.
CLINTON ST.
FULTON ST.
ATLANTIC AVE.
STATE ST.
JORALEMON ST.
GRACE CT.
REMSEN ST.
MONTAGUE ST.
PIERREPONT ST.
CLARK ST.
PINEAPPLE ST.
ORANGE ST.
CRANBERRY ST.
LIVINGSTON ST.
PLYMOUTH CHURCH
PART OF WARD I
SECTION I
Scale 100 Feet to the Inch.

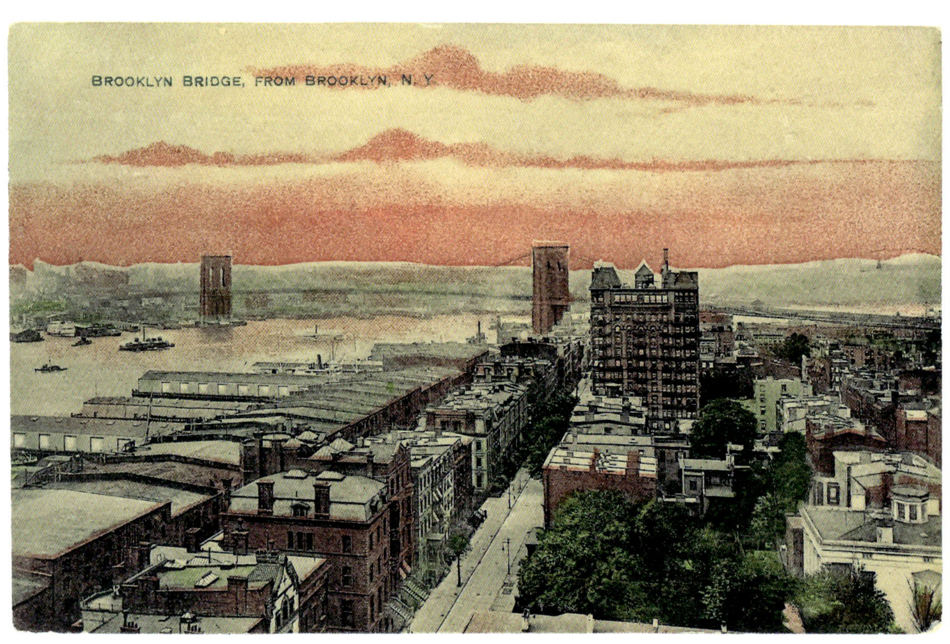
BROOKLYN BRIDGE, FROM BROOKLYN, N. Y.

Fig. 7
Map of Brooklyn Heights, annotated to show Hamilton Easter Field's home at 106 Columbia Heights. Published by E. B. Hyde & Co., 1903–7. Lionel Pincus and Princess Firyal Map Division, New York Public Library

Fig. 8
"Brooklyn Bridge, from Brooklyn, N.Y.," postcard showing the Brooklyn Heights neighborhood, with its main street of Columbia Heights in the foreground, ca. 1910. The Bob Stonehill Postcard Collection

prominent location and larger-than-average lot size, the house projected an air of modesty and simplicity. A hybrid of Federal and Greek Revival architectural styles, the building was a typical row house, its design sourced from a builder's guide (fig. 10).[49] The three-bay facade of the Field house was articulated in exposed brick, and the low-relief trim on the windows, front door, and cornices was either brownstone or granite. The building was sixty feet (or just over eighteen meters) deep, and due to the sloping nature of the site, it gained extra stories at the rear. As a result, the back was structured differently from the front: it had five stories above ground plus an attic. The rear facade also included a protruding trapezoidal bay with side windows that extended along the building's full height (fig. 11). While typical row houses at first glance, 106 and the neighboring properties that made up Quaker Row were nevertheless architectural, or more precisely, engineering, anomalies. The property owners jointly developed their sloping back gardens into four-story warehouses with entrances on Furman Street, which ran below and to the west of Columbia Heights. As a result, the Quaker Row properties consisted of two independent structures: the roofs of the warehouses fronting Furman Street served as the back gardens of the row houses on Columbia Heights.[50]

When, in 1902, after nearly eight years in Europe, Field packed up his Parisian studio on rue de Seine in the city's Latin Quarter and relocated to his native Brooklyn, he began to put his stamp on the house, which he shared with his widowed mother, Lydia Seaman Haviland Field (who was also the legal owner of the property).[51] Over time various parts of the house began to reflect his wide-ranging tastes in art and interest in interior design; the paintings and sculpture, drawings and prints, and decorative arts and antique furniture he amassed while in Europe were integrated into the home's original, old-fashioned decor. Field began making these changes piecemeal, targeting specific areas of the house.[52]

By 1905 he had completed an extensive renovation on the third floor, transforming the original bedrooms located there into a bachelor's suite with an artist studio rendered in the image of his Parisian quarters (but far more generous in size). According to the Brooklyn press, Field's domain began in the stairwell leading to the third-floor landing, its walls hung with art and lined with art books. The primary space—taking up half of the entire floor area—was a large, L-shaped painting studio and gallery situated at the back

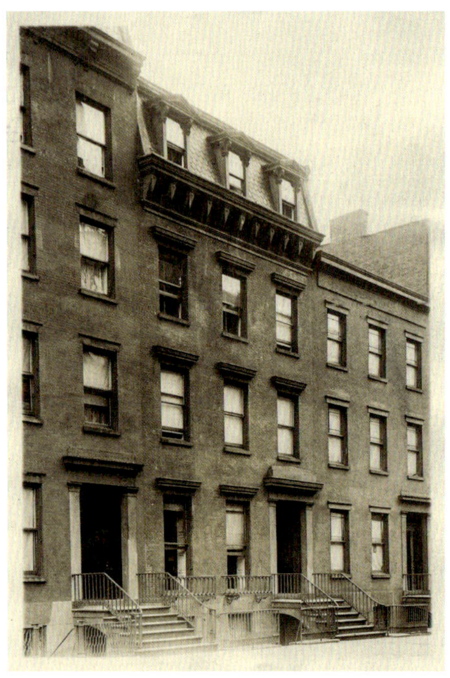

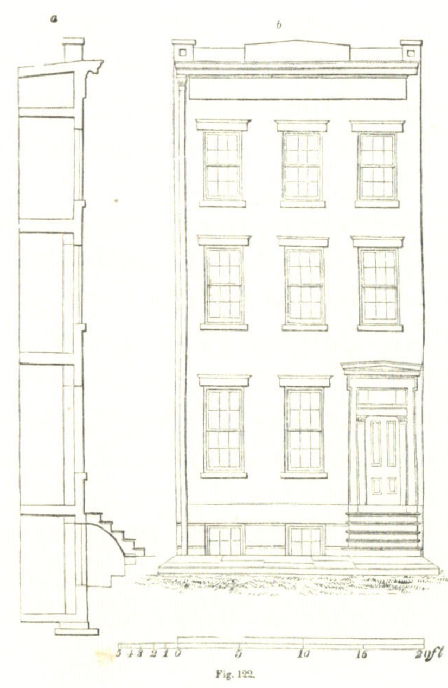

Fig. 9
Eugene L. Armbruster, *Brooklyn: Roebling House, 110 Columbia Heights, between Orange Street and Pineapple Street*, 1922. [Armbruster incorrectly noted the location as Pineapple Street instead of Cranberry Street. Field's home, 106 Columbia Heights, is at far right.] New-York Historical Society, Eugene L. Armbruster Photograph Collection, 1894–1939

Fig. 10
Page 95 from R. [Robert] G. [Griffith] Hatfield's *The American House-Carpenter: A Treatise upon Architecture, Cornices and Mouldings, Framing, Doors, Windows, and Stairs. Together with the Most Important Principles of Practical Geometry* (1845), showing an elevation and cross section of an "ordinary city house"

Fig. 11
View of the rear facade of 106 Columbia Heights, at center, with protruding trapezoidal bay, ca. 1946. Roebling Collection, Archives and Special Collections, Folsom Library, Rensselaer Polytechnic Institute, Troy, N.Y.

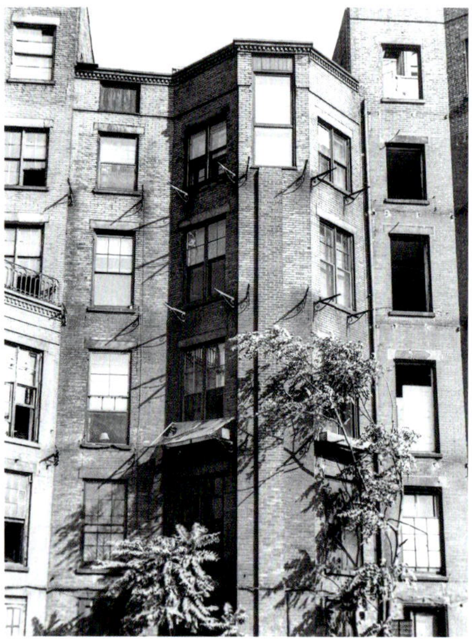

of the house that was achieved by the removal of partition walls (fig. 12).[53] It was designed to display Field's extensive and eclectic art collection, antique furniture, and examples of decorative arts from Europe and elsewhere. The studio-gallery was connected to a "half cupboard, half adjoining room," or an alcove, for storing an easel and canvases, its entrance marked by two spiral gilded columns. Field opened the already spacious room's interior to the outside by installing a double-height west-facing window within the protruding portion of the back facade. According to Mary Berenson, one of the many visitors ushered to Field's studio over the years, the panoramic view of the East River and the Manhattan skyline from the window was the "most amazing and enthralling spectacle" she and her husband, Bernard, "ever had experienced."[54] Paul Haviland captured the vista with his camera during a visit to the house (fig. 13).[55]

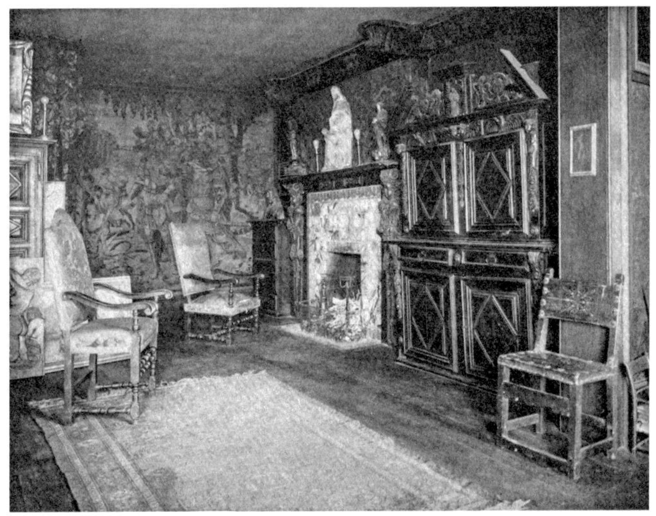

Fig. 12
Field's third-floor studio at 106 Columbia Heights, Brooklyn, published in *International Studio* 54, no. 233 (July 1916)

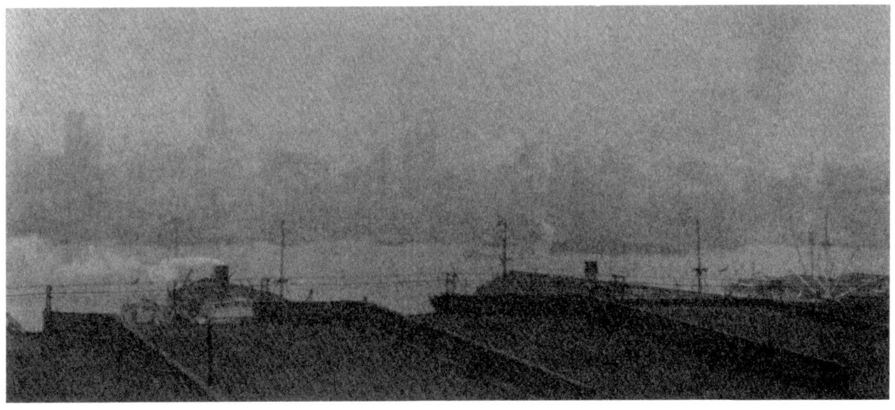

Fig. 13
Paul Haviland, *View of Brooklyn Bridge and Manhattan from the Field residence at 106 Columbia Heights*, before 1910. Platinum proof, 4 × 5 in. (10.2 × 12.5 cm). Musée d'Orsay, Fonds Paul Burty Haviland (PHO 1993 1 76)

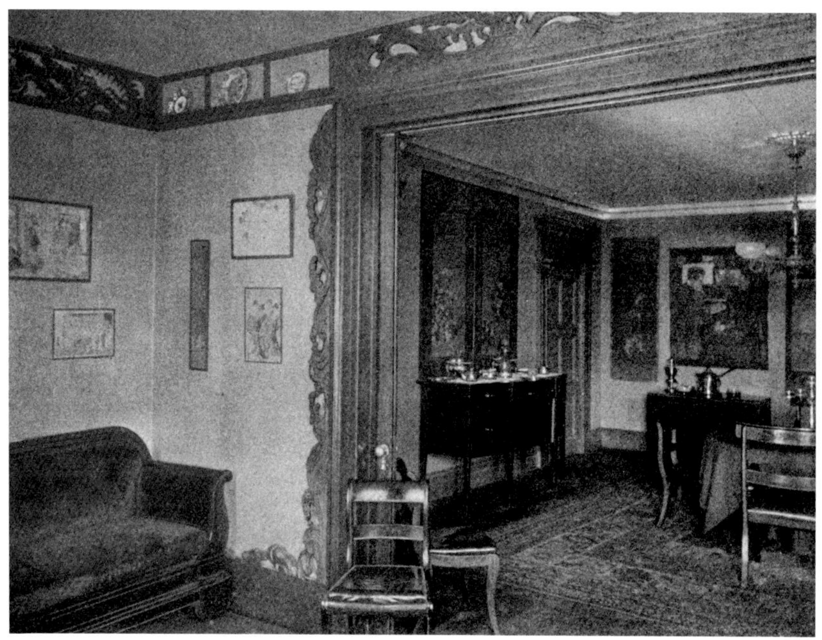

Fig. 14
The Unique Japanese Breakfast-Room in the Field House, *Brooklyn Life*, February 17, 1906. Brooklyn Public Library, Center for Brooklyn History

Field did not confine his interest in the interior alterations of the house to the third floor. In 1906 *Brooklyn Life* published photographs of the newly renovated rear drawing room and breakfast room of the Field residence—both spaces likely located on one of the lower levels below the parlor floor (fig. 14). These rooms attest to Field's ongoing effort to improve the aesthetic quality of the interiors.[56] For this update, Field drew inspiration from traditional Japanese architectural interiors and his extensive Japanese print collection assembled in Paris.[57] He covered the walls with Japanese grass cloth and further embellished them with carved wooden panels and hanging scrolls. Omitted from public coverage, on the other hand, was Field's fitting of one of the subterranean levels of the house with a spacious bathing facility modeled on ancient Roman *thermae*, which featured tilework that emanated "an Oriental feeling."[58] The exact location of this space within the house and the date of this interior remodeling has not been thus far determined.

In 1909 Field turned his attention to the parlor floor of the house, which boasted generously sized double reception rooms off the entry hallway and central staircase, as well as a smaller room positioned behind the staircase and accessed from the hallway and the back parlor. This is the space Field offered to Picasso. With no floor plans of the house in existence, the confirmation of this location derives from yet another decorative commission for the house. Robert Laurent, who resided at 106 together with Field and Field's mother on a permanent basis as of around 1910, was enlisted by Field to design and carve a suite of furniture and walnut decorative fittings for his mother's second-floor bedroom. The latter included a fireplace decoration consisting of a series of panels carved in low relief (fig. 15). The topmost horizontal panel depicting a scene with hot-air balloons also features references to the architecture of the house: a cross section of the aforementioned subterranean bathing chamber, at far left, and the floor plans of the second and parlor stories, at far right (fig. 16). Laurent used Latin terms to identify the functions or occupancy of the rooms; for instance, the double parlors were *Bibliotheca Agrorum* or, in literal translation, the Library of Field. The room Field allocated to Picasso was identified as the *Bibliothecula*, or Small Library. Also indicated on the plan for the parlor floor were two fireplaces, some large pieces of furniture, and a grand piano with an accompanying stool. These interconnected spaces hosted well-attended public concerts, lectures, receptions, and recitals, which received coverage in the Brooklyn press.[59]

The 1913 floor plan of Laurent's *Bibliothecula* panel aligns with that in Field's letter in all but one detail (see detail of fig. 16). The Field-drawn plan had indicated a third door, marked C, positioned across from the one leading to the back parlor. This was either a nonfunctional blind door original to the building's initial design and installed to achieve symmetry, or alternatively, it indicated a future alteration. By 1905 Field had acquired the house next door at 104 Columbia Heights, which he used as an income-generating rental property. It is conceivable that Field envisioned building a passageway between the two properties in due course. As evidenced from Laurent's relief, such a connector did not exist as of 1913.

Reading Field's letter, with its lack of demands, Picasso would have considered it his good fortune in finding a hands-off patron. Picasso enjoyed full creative autonomy, as confirmed by Field in his letter: "As you know, in any case I give you complete freedom." (See pp. 90–91 for a reproduction of the letter.) Yet, the patron did reiterate the project's decorative nature, emphasizing that Picasso's paintings needed to comply with a particular architectural space. Field used the words *panneau/panneaux* (panel/panels) when referring to Picasso's future works, avoiding altogether terms reserved for easel painting such as *tableau* (easel painting), *toile* (canvas), or *peinture* (painting). At the same time, Field downplayed the room's existing style, implying that the full and final effect of the space was entirely in Picasso's hands.

Fig. 15
Fireplace in a Bedroom in Mrs. Aaron Field's Residence, 106 Columbia Heights (wood paneling by Robert Laurent and painting by Hamilton Easter Field), *Brooklyn Life*, March 27, 1915. Brooklyn Public Library, Center for Brooklyn History

Fig. 16
Robert Laurent, *Balloons*, 1913. Walnut, 9 × 65¾ × ⅞ in. (22.8 × 167 × 2.2 cm). Private collection

Detail of fig. 16, showing the far-right section with the floor plans of the second (at top) and parlor (at bottom) stories

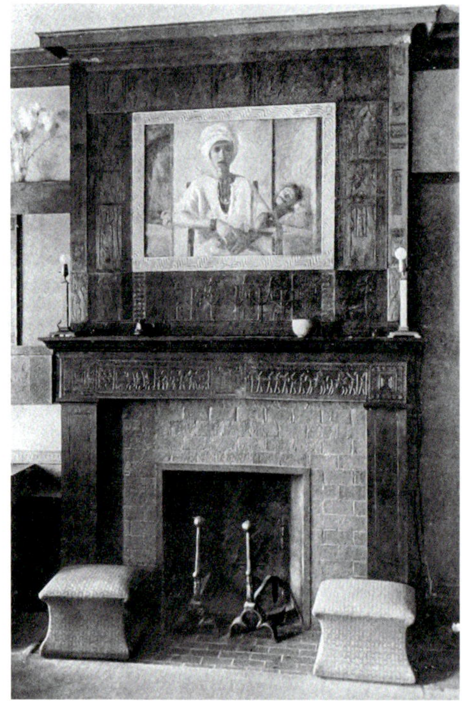

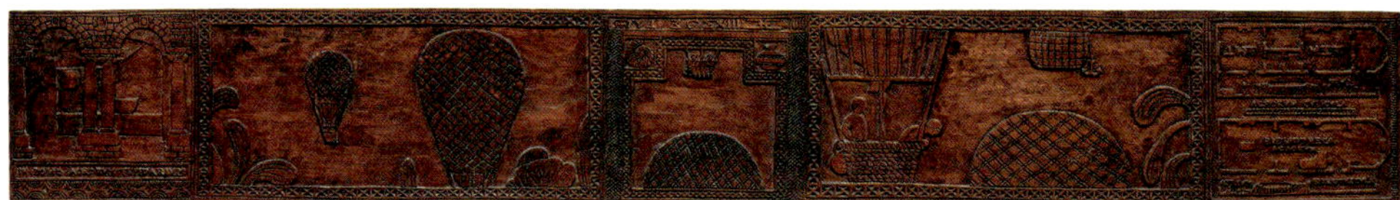

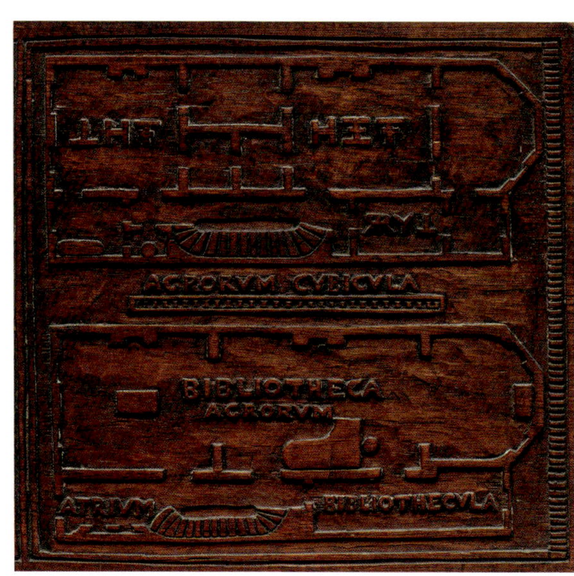

THE LARGE PANEL FOR AMERICA

When did Picasso actually begin the Field commission? The answer remains tantalizingly speculative. The artist responded to his patron's letter on September 1 once back in Paris. His communication, also in French, was curt and noncommittal, offering only an acknowledgment of Field's letter and his intention of starting the commission in the near future (for a reproduction of the letter and a full translation, see the Chronology section on p. 92).[60]

Pencil annotations consisting of "I" and "X" marks, presumably made by Picasso, can be found on Field's diagram in six of the eight rectangular wall areas (each representing a different wall size). When they were made and what they signified for the artist remain unclear. On the basis of stylistic evidence, however, it appears that Picasso first turned his attention to the narrow, vertical wall areas E and H and chose the standing female figure as subject matter. In his catalogue raisonné of Picasso's Cubist years, Pierre Daix dated the start of both *Nude Woman* (pl. 1) and *Woman with a Fan* (pl. 15) to summer 1910, when, in Cadaqués, Picasso embarked on a group of radically abstract figure compositions. Be it in oil on canvas or graphic media, Picasso disrupted the boundaries between bodies and space by abandoning the continuous contour line and reducing the figure to a series of lines and curves with the barest analogies to actual anatomy. His use of piecemeal shading to suggest fluctuating light and fragmented volume, as well as a subtly gradated color palette, contributed to the paintings' varying degrees of illegibility.

A photograph published by Richardson in the context of the commission purportedly captures Picasso's Cadaqués studio that summer filled with a group of canvases, including a large vertical-format composition, unstretched and tacked to the wall (fig. 17).[61] Whether this painting was lost or destroyed, or was an earlier version of one of the extant Field panels, remains unknown, even as Picasso, decades later, apparently claimed to Daix that he had begun both *Nude Woman* and *Woman with a Fan* in Cadaqués.[62] Instead, it is worth considering that Picasso would have had limited time between his receipt of Field's letter in Cadaqués after August 2, his six-day visit to Barcelona (from August 6 to 12), and his return to Paris on the 26th of that month. Would the artist have started to paint or waited until he could consider the number and sizes of canvases and their interrelationships, once back in his permanent studio? Despite his claims to Daix, Picasso's letter to Field suggests the latter. Regardless, and perhaps more telling, Kahnweiler considered the pictures that Picasso brought back from Cadaqués to be unfinished.

The dimensions of *Nude Woman* (73¾ by 24 inches, or 187.3 by 61 centimeters) most closely match wall space E, which is 70 centimeters wide

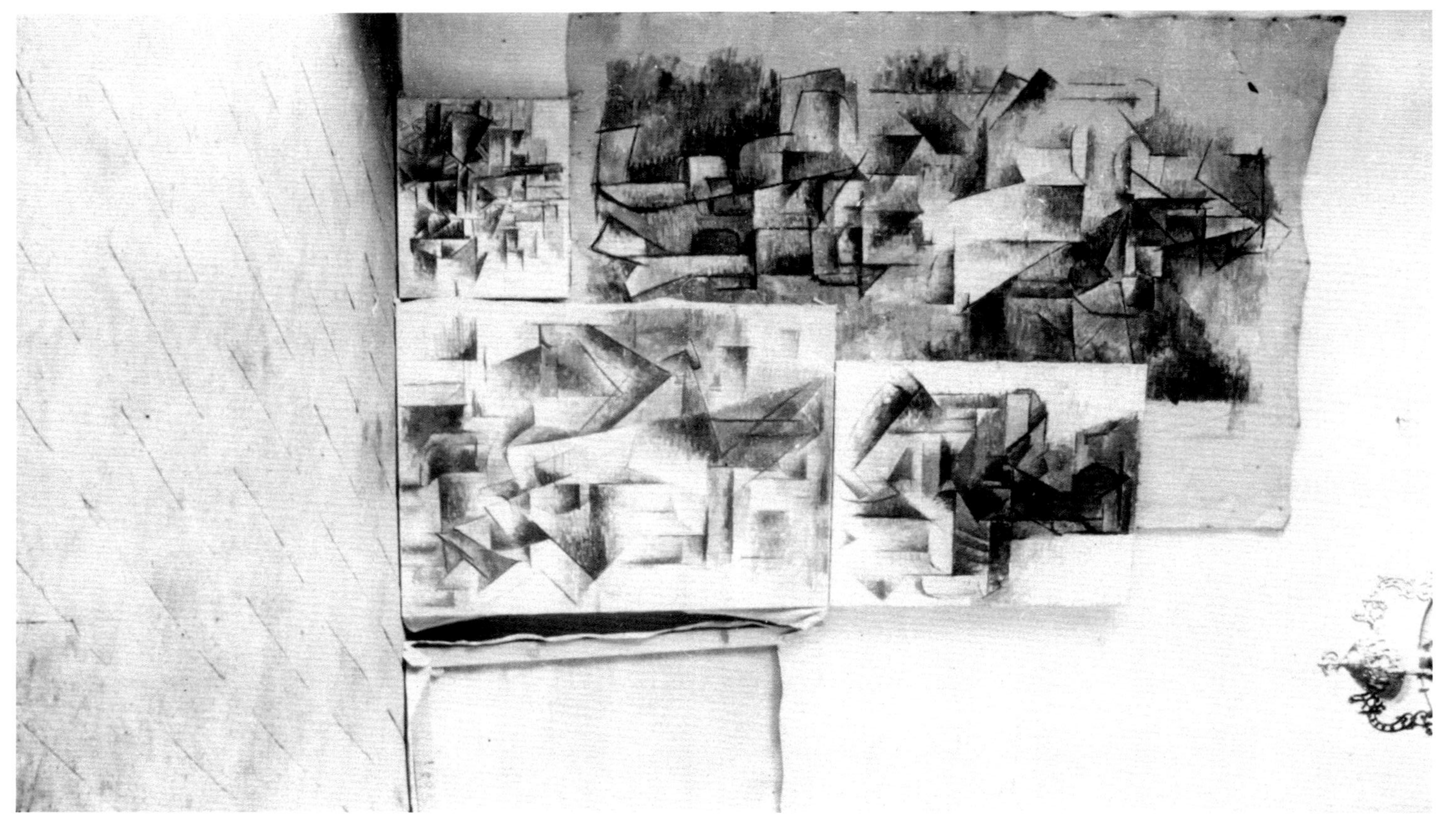

Fig. 17
Picasso's studio, Cadaqués, Spain, 1910. Reversed original print. Private collection

and adjacent to door B. The width of the painting comes 3⅝ inches (9 centimeters) short of the wall's available width, and its height is about ⅞ inch (2 centimeters) longer than the stipulated wall height of 72⅞ inches (185 centimeters). The dimensions of *Woman with a Fan* (72⅞ by 28⅝ inches, or 185 by 72.5 centimeters) make it the most likely candidate for wall space H, next to the library's large window. Like *Nude Woman*, it is also narrower than the allotted space, in this instance, by about 1 inch (2.5 centimeters). In both cases Picasso might have been anticipating a need for a framing device such as a wooden strip or molding around the margins of the canvas once in situ, so that the works would be set flush with the wall.

These two large paintings belong to Picasso's prolonged interrogation of the standing female figure in an orthogonal gridlike format throughout 1910, notably in works on paper. That the artist executed these sketches in a variety of mediums—pen and ink, charcoal, or watercolor—vividly demonstrates the important role drawing played in his creative process. He made many of them on relatively narrow sheets undoubtedly chosen to accentuate the vertical stance of the figures. His earliest investigations date to spring 1910, when he began producing large drawings, among them *Female Nude* (pl. 2). During the summer in Cadaqués, he generated a closely related series of pen-and-ink drawings—among them *Standing Nude* (fig. 18), *Standing Nude* (pl. 3), *Standing Female Nude* (pl. 4), and *Nude* (pl. 5). At the same moment, he was conceiving the illustrations for *Saint Matorel*, a book written by his friend Max Jacob. Two of these images also depict the female figure in a vertical format.[63] The large-scale charcoal drawing titled *Standing Female Nude*, noted for its abstract characteristics, is dated to the latter part of 1910 (pl. 7).

Displaying a variety of shading techniques, these sheets offer instructive counterpoints for *Nude Woman* and the first stage of *Woman with a Fan*. Each represents a specific moment in Picasso's development of a new geometric language to represent human anatomy.[64] No preparatory works for the Field panels exist per se, though Picasso did complete a small related oil, *Standing Nude Woman*, in Cadaqués or back in Paris (pl. 6). Recent technical analysis of this painted sketch undertaken by the conservator Emilie Faust revealed that Picasso likely used a prestretched commercially prepared canvas and proceeded without his usual charcoal underdrawing.[65] The overall impression is that of a quickly jotted-down idea, in contrast to the carefully plotted works on paper. Despite the painting's diminutive scale—smaller than many of the works on paper mentioned above—and its being slightly more representational than the more than six-foot-long *Nude*

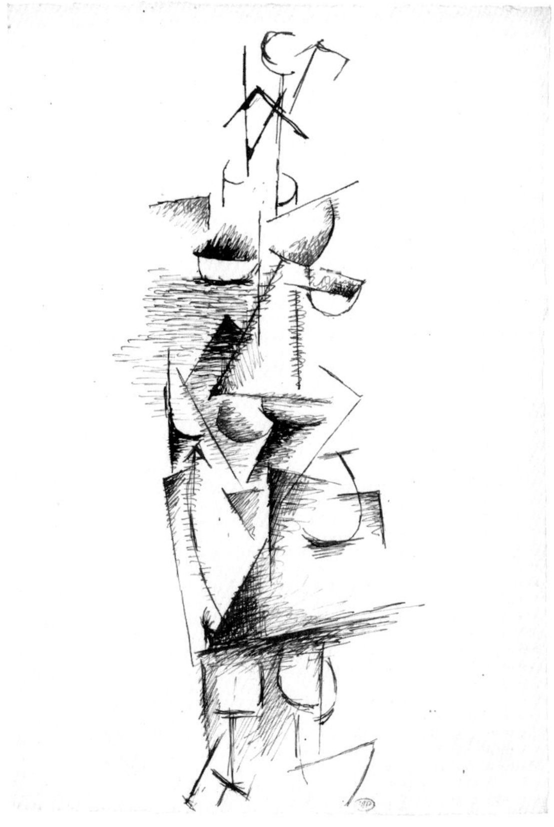

Fig. 18
Pablo Picasso, *Standing Nude*, summer 1910. Pen and India ink on pale green paper, 12 ½ × 8 ½ in. (31.6 × 21.5 cm). Musée National Picasso-Paris (MP 645)

Woman, the oil sketch and the oil painting nevertheless attest to the emergence of Picasso's new Cubist syntax of human anatomy.

At first glance the fully realized painting *Nude Woman* gives the impression of a uniform composition; however, there are few clues within the work to corroborate its titular subject as either a nude or a female. Derived from the earth tones of burnt umber and black, the dominant palette reinforces the initial overall effect of formal continuity. Lengthier examination, however, reveals the painting's division into three distinct zones. In the upper third, corresponding to the figure's head and chest, Picasso opted for dramatic value contrast, approaching the human physiognomy almost like a still life, more a collection of geometrized things than an overall faceted volume. The rhythmic control demonstrated in this section of the painting evokes that of the pen-and-ink drawings from Cadaqués. The effect of such treatment results in the slowing down of the viewer's eye as it moves over the pictorial form. In the painting's midsection, which can be described as its most active zone, Picasso reduced the value contrast but amplified the density of paint application, increased the visibility of individual brushstrokes, and expanded the color palette through the localized use of burnt sienna, Naples yellow, and an earthy green. In the painting's bottom third, the artist softened the paint application to a washy scrub. Unlike the upper two-thirds of the painting, where line defines the outer edge of the picture plane, line in the lowest third is reduced to a skeletal framework of increasingly large planes scarcely corresponding to local shifts in value and hue. The apparent lack of resolve at the bottom of the work gives the figure a sense of weightlessness and disconnection to the ground—unusual elements for a full-length figure painting. This portion of the work likely contributed to the evaluation of *Nude Woman* by leading scholars, among them Cubist specialist Douglas Cooper, as unfinished.[66] Compared to *Nude Woman*, *Woman with a Fan* is similarly sized. Although Picasso later reworked it in a different Cubist style in 1918, the overall quality of its first state and its formal similarities to *Nude Woman* are still visible. According to a 1948 description, the underlying painting of *Woman with a Fan* "breaks up the forms of the human figure into a series of planes set at angles and rendered in delicate touches of near monochrome."[67] Unfortunately, the lack of opportunity to directly examine this complex painting prevents adequate evaluation.

In 1989, in his quest to match Picasso's paintings with the Field commission specifications, Rubin became convinced that *Man with a Guitar* and *Man with a Mandolin* (both Musée National Picasso-Paris) (pls. 8, 9) also belonged to the commission, proposing that Picasso produced them after becoming dissatisfied with *Nude Woman* and *Woman with a Fan*. They represented a corrective to the pictorial and formal problems of the earlier two. In Rubin's own words: "One has only to compare the two pairs [*Nude Woman* and *Woman with a Fan* versus *Man with a Guitar* and *Man with a Mandolin*] to see how much more harmonious and workable the new proportions are."[68] To reach this conclusion, Rubin put aside his own logical criteria of matching Picasso's works with the commission based on their dimensions. The heights and widths of *Man with a Guitar* (60⅝ by 30½ inches, or 154 by 77.5 centimeters) and *Man with a Mandolin* (63⅞ by 28 inches, or 162 by 71 centimeters) do not meet the measurements prescribed by Field. Nevertheless, it is likely that these two works and their particular spatial and compositional features were indeed born of—if not directly made for—the commission and Picasso's exploration of two key issues introduced in the 1910 summer at Cadaqués: the infiltration of bodies with the surrounding space and the limits of legibility.

Man with a Guitar and *Man with a Mandolin* have complex histories, parts of which have been brought to light by Pepe Karmel.[69] According to Karmel, Picasso initially executed these two paintings in the spring of 1911.

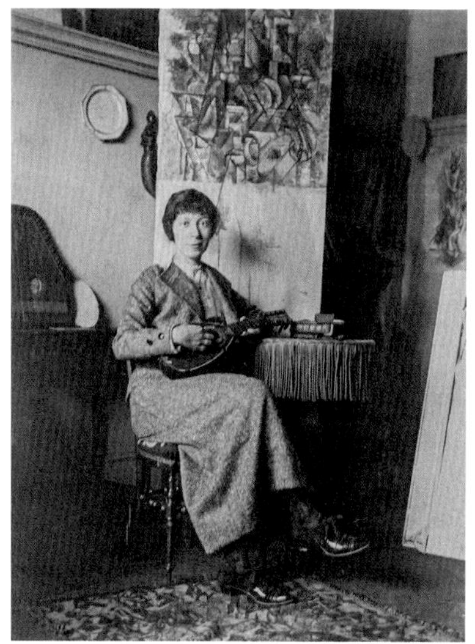

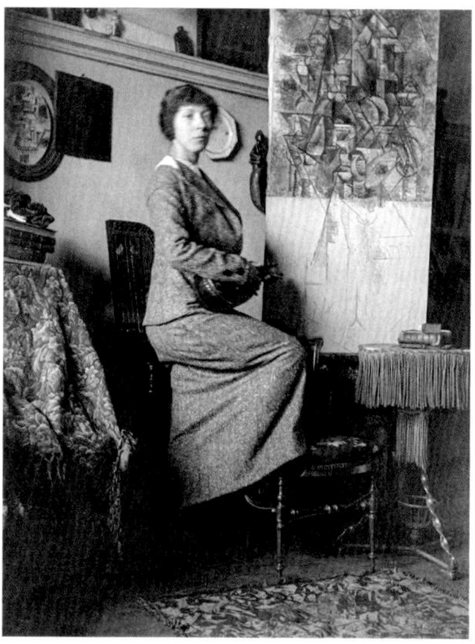

Fig. 19
Marie Laurencin sitting next to *Man with a Mandolin* (pl. 9) in progress, in Picasso's boulevard de Clichy studio, Paris, fall 1911. Fundación Almine y Bernard Ruiz-Picasso para el Arte, Madrid

Fig. 20
Marie Laurencin standing next to *Man with a Mandolin* (pl. 9) in Picasso's boulevard de Clichy studio, Paris, fall 1911. Picasso Archives, Musée National Picasso-Paris

Both started out as easel-size and represented half-length figures of a musician.[70] Picasso returned to these paintings in the fall of 1911 and extended the length of each work, nearly doubling their heights. In the case of *Man with a Guitar*, that involved unfolding an additional length of the canvas the artist had initially tucked behind the painting, whereas for *Man with a Mandolin* he added a new piece of canvas along the bottom.[71] Two archival photographs dated to fall 1911 show Picasso's artist friend Marie Laurencin both seated and standing next to *Man with a Mandolin*. At this stage it had already been extended, but only a delineated composition in the added portion was depicted (figs. 19, 20). Laurencin holds the titular stringed instrument, and her posed stances suggest the two-dimensional "man" in the adjacent painting is rendered also either sitting or standing.

Notably, one major drawing, *Standing Woman,* was similarly extended (pl. 10). Composed of two joined sheets of paper, it shares with the paintings an analogous horizontal seam just below the midpoint mark. Though traditionally dated to the summer of 1912, *Standing Woman* has a direct relationship to the paintings of the same subject executed during the summer of 1910 in Cadaqués. Picasso used a variety of media—ink, charcoal dipped in oil, and gouache—as if applying different textures, tones, and transparent planes to simulate the equivalent strokes, stippling, and light-dark modulations of the paintings.

In both *Man with a Guitar* and *Man with a Mandolin*, Picasso labored to quiet the horizontal crease and seam, respectively, loading the upper portions with visual incident in the form of small multifaceted planes of color carefully recording a left-hand light source. The upper section of *Man with a Mandolin* is composed of an intricate web of straight and curved lines. The figure and background seamlessly intertwine to form a single continuous vibrant surface. In *Man with a Guitar*, which Picasso continued to work on as late as 1913, a blocklike figure emerges from the densely packed background. For both paintings, the bottom portion of the composition, while continuous with the upper section in terms of color and intersecting forms, sees a reduction in complexity as well as a lightening in value. In *Man with a Mandolin* the lower extension reflects the process used for the upper portion by way of a gradual stacking of planes. Tying the painting back to props in his studio, Picasso painted the mobilizing feature of the wheels of Laurencin's chair. In *Man with a Guitar* the lower portion of the painting is composed of broad vertical planes of differing hues. In both compositions, the overall tone lightens at the base, as is also seen in *Nude Woman* of 1910, imparting a sense of airiness that mitigates the gravitational pull of full-length compositions.

Further complicating an assessment of the Field commission is a photograph, dated 1913, of Picasso's studio at 242 boulevard Raspail in Montparnasse (fig. 21). It documents another work of comparable subject and size, leaning against another, even larger work. Depicting a figure seated in an armchair, the composition in the photograph shares with *Man with a Guitar* and *Man with a Mandolin* stylistic characteristics such as the dichotomy of a densely developed upper portion and a lighter lower section. Naturalistically rendered details such as the curve of the furniture's armrest or the wheels of the chair are similar to elements in *Man with a Mandolin*.[72] The scale and proportions of this work, however, are akin to the 1910 oblong paintings, especially *Woman with a Fan*. Because the painting recorded in the photographs has yet to be identified, its dimensions can only be approximated based on comparisons with the other painting visible in the photograph, *The Soler Family* (1903; Musée des Beaux-Arts, Liège), which measures 59 ⅛ by 78 ¾ inches (150 by 200 centimeters). Picasso was in the process of repainting this work as of spring 1913.[73] The photograph, linked to the commission by Richardson, indicates Picasso's continued engagement with the project. This documentary photograph also brings new meaning to the clause Picasso included in his December 1912 contract with Kahnweiler, in which he stipulated retaining the right to accept commissions for "large decorations destined for a specific place"—likely made

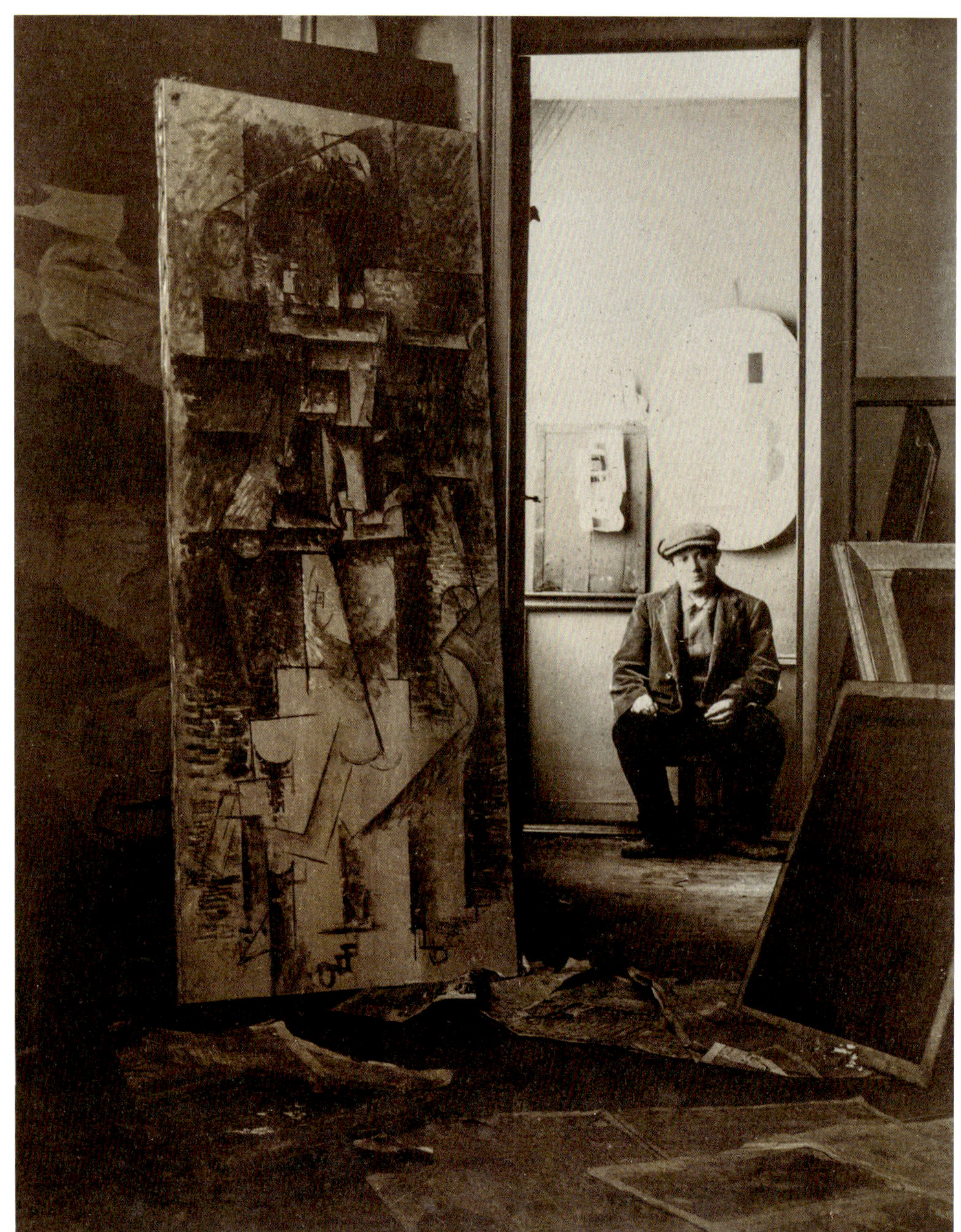

Fig. 21
Pablo Picasso in his boulevard Raspail studio, Paris, 1913. Picasso Archives, Musée National Picasso-Paris

Fig. 22
Pablo Picasso in his studio at 11 boulevard de Clichy, Paris, late 1911. Picasso Archives, Musée National Picasso-Paris

in reference to the Field project, which he was continuing to work on.[74]

The documentary photograph that Rubin considered in his 1989 account of the Field commission is that of Picasso's boulevard de Clichy studio dated to the latter half of 1911 (fig. 22). In it is a partially visible, still unaccounted for, and presumably destroyed mural-size painting. Rubin identified this large composition as a candidate for one of the four large rectangular wall panels specified in Field's letter. Mining archival materials for any additional clues, Rubin hypothesized that this painting was the work mentioned in Picasso's July 25, 1911, letter to his then close friend and artistic confidant Georges Braque. Writing from the town of Céret in the French Pyrenees while awaiting Braque's arrival there, Picasso reported working on the pastoral scene of "the big painting" in the spacious studio made available to him by none other than Frank Burty Haviland.[75] In addition, Rubin believed that this was the same painting as the one described by the artist as "le grand paneau [*sic*] pour l'Amérique" (the large panel for America) and listed as number twenty-three in the inventory of Picasso's unfinished works stored at the auxiliary rue Ravignan studio at Bateau-Lavoir dated June 5, 1912.[76] In Rubin's hypothetical reconstruction of events, when Picasso left Céret to arrive in Paris by early September, he took the painting with him to Paris and tacked it to a

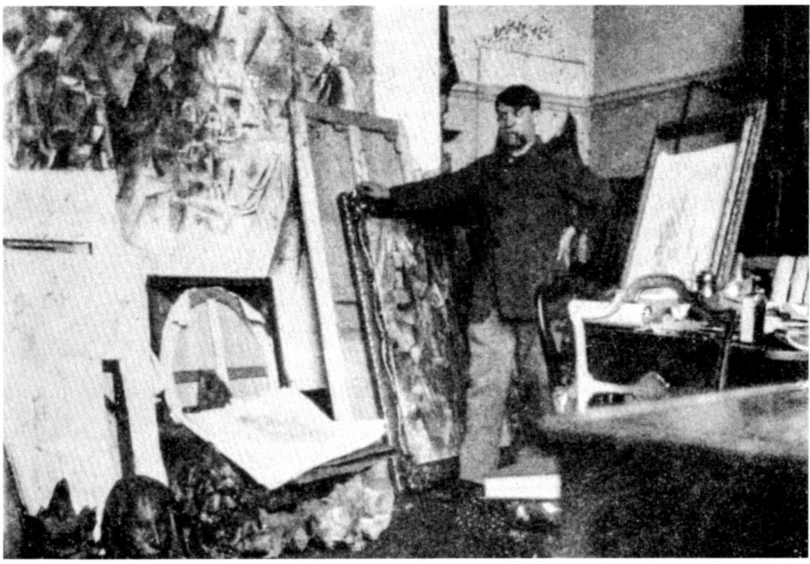

wall of his studio, presumably to continue working on it. By the time the photograph was taken, the artist had stacked other paintings against it, making the subject matter of this mural-size canvas virtually impossible to identify. Picasso's indifferent treatment of the work suggests that it no longer held his primary focus when the photograph was taken.[77] The 1912 inventory indicates that the work was relegated to storage possibly not long after the photograph was taken.

As Picasso attended to the standing nude throughout 1910, he also rendered the occasional reclining female figure, despite it being a rare subject within Picasso's Cubist period on the whole. One of these works is *Reclining Nude*, a small horizontal painting from spring 1910 (fig. 23). In documentary photographs from fall–winter 1910, Picasso and some of his visitors in the artist's boulevard de Clichy studio are shown with this image hung on a wall amid a selection of his works and those by other artists. Among them was a reproduction of Jean Auguste Dominique Ingres's *Grande Odalisque* (1814; Musée du Louvre). Picasso had installed his *Reclining Nude* kitty-corner from one of his contemporaneous large drawings of standing female figures. At some point Picasso exchanged one drawing for another. According to one photograph,[78] for a time Picasso paired *Reclining Nude* with one of his large drawings dated to spring 1910, while other photos show the painting similarly paired with the large charcoal drawing *Standing Female Nude* (pl. 7) pinned to the wall unframed (fig. 24).[79] The juxtaposition of these two motifs, executed on nearly identical scale and with the same degree of abstraction, reveals that Picasso was intrigued by the compositional changes entailed with switching orientation.

Indeed, at the time these photographs were taken, Picasso had likely already embarked on his first horizontal picture for the commission, *Reclining Woman on a Sofa* (pl. 11). Daix dated it to fall 1910, acknowledging its stylistic affinity with the works of the Cadaqués period. Despite shared subject matter, the large horizontal canvas is a decisive departure from the small *Reclining Nude*, particularly in the way Picasso handled the figure/ground relation. In *Reclining Nude* the woman's body, placed parallel to the picture plane, is set forth from its surroundings by an intensification of interior cross-contour lines and a shift to lighter values within the body.[80] Such clarity is nonexistent in the large *Reclining Woman on a Sofa*. The subject matter of this work is as legible (or, rather, as illegible) as its vertical pendant, *Nude Woman* (pl. 1), painted around the same time. Tending toward dematerialization, the allover composition offers no central focal point to draw the viewer's eye. Intersecting diagonals zigzag across the picture plane, weaving in and out of stacked rectangular volumes that constitute both body and space, encouraging a read of the panel as abstract and perceptually elusive. To

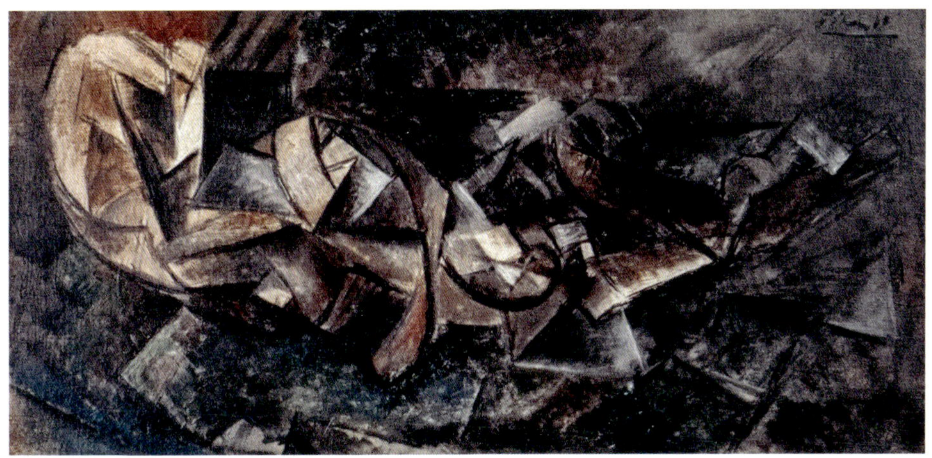

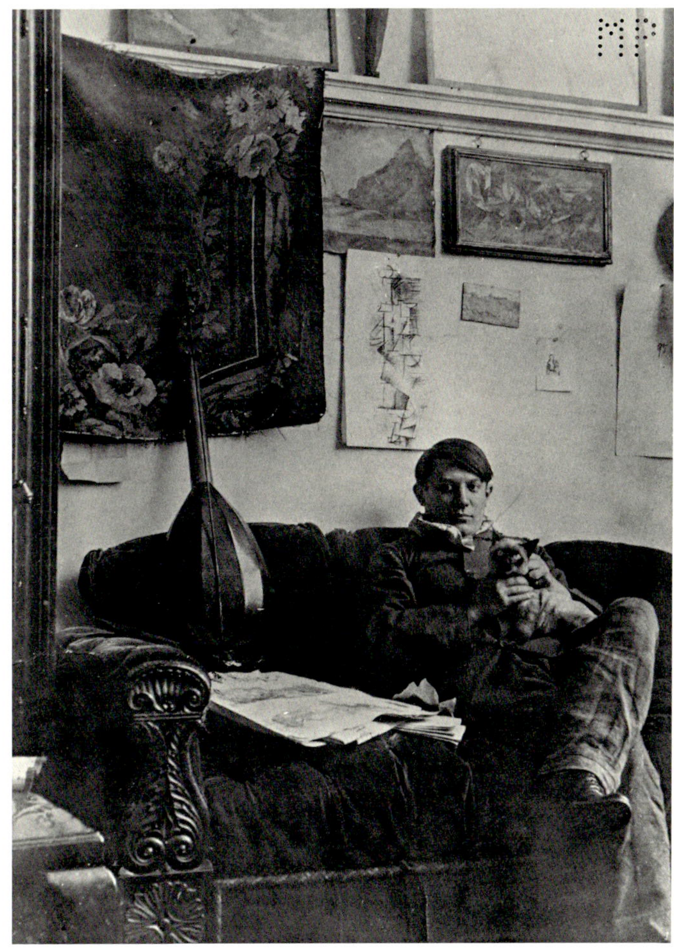

Fig. 23
Pablo Picasso, *Reclining Nude,* spring 1910. Oil on canvas, 8¾ × 18⅛ in. (22 × 46 cm). Private collection, Japan

Fig. 24
Pablo Picasso in his studio at 11 boulevard de Clichy, with the unframed *Standing Female Nude* (pl. 7) shown behind him and *Reclining Nude* (fig. 23) above right, December 1910. Gelatin silver print, 9⅜ × 6¾ in. (23.3 × 17.1 cm). Picasso Archives, Musée National Picasso-Paris (MPPH15330)

achieve a sense of visual balance, Picasso divided the picture into two near-equal zones. On the left side, heightened value contrasts and spatial recession impart a sense of drama, whereas the more serene right side features large forms in paler hues that more evenly conform to the picture plane.

The title of the work and the orientation of the brushstrokes come to the viewer's aid; the pairing of lines and shapes together forms a schematic representation of a reclining female figure in an indoor setting.[81] The diagonals suggest, from left to right, a bent arm, a thigh, a lower leg, and a foot. The curves in the vicinity of each diagonal redirection can be read as rounded body parts: a shoulder, buttocks, a knee, and a heel. The furniture referenced in the artwork's title is indicated on the far left by the elegant volute of a sofa's armrest.

Field's brief called for three horizontal overdoor paintings of identical dimensions (19¾ by 51¼ inches, or 50 by 130 centimeters) to mark the room's three doorways; these would be viewed from below and at an angle. Since gaining popularity in France in the seventeenth century, *dessus de porte* (literally, "over the door") panels executed for the same room typically adhered to a common theme or subject matter. Historically, decorative painting ensembles were dictated by the designated wall area of the room. They consisted of the mural-size compositions intended for primary areas, as well as slim vertical side panels and narrow horizontal overdoors, which filled secondary wall sections. These ancillary panels were not well-suited to multi-figure compositions and instead were complementary to a narrative or an allegorical ensemble. Hence, draped or nude female figures, in slight or full contrapposto, were a preferred choice for vertical sidebars. Typically pictured standing on a plinth or framed by a niche, they often filled the elongated vertical format. Alternatively, these vertical formats showcased floral or still-life pattern compositions. Reclining figures or still lifes proved suitable for the horizontal format of the overdoors. Picasso would have certainly been familiar with the convention, initially settling on the reclining female figure as his overarching subject for the three overdoors of the Field commission. As the first of the three overdoors, it is reasonable to speculate that Picasso likely intended *Reclining Woman on a Sofa*, which measures 19⅜ by 51 inches (49 by 129.5 centimeters), for the space above doorway A. Notably, it was the last painting of a reclining figure that Picasso carried out during his Cubist years.

Faced with similarly challenging formats for the Field commission, Picasso conformed to the decorative painting tradition embraced by such artists as Auguste Renoir. Like Maurice Denis, Renoir was strongly influenced by Italian Renaissance frescoes and set out to modernize decorative painting.[82] From the 1880s onward, he repeatedly chose exaggerated vertical and horizontal formats depicting both standing and reclining figures. A great number of these paintings, among them *Large Nude* of 1907 (fig. 25) and the pair of paintings titled *Caryatids* of around 1910 (figs. 26, 27), were executed without a commission of predetermined and fixed destination. Renoir turned to caryatids (female figures meant to serve as architectural support) as subject matter, exploiting the compressed space to accentuate the sensual curves of the female form, from the exaggerated buttocks of contrapposto stance to the display of the breasts ostensibly necessitated by the upheld garlands. Picasso avoids this overt sensuality, instead preferring subtle rhythmic shifts and moody tones. Moreover, he suppresses any references to attributes or fictional architectural settings in which figures typically stand. Nonetheless, once familiar with the variety in this tradition, one might note the kinship of his monochromatic value range with the grisaille palette, employed for imitating stone statues or reliefs, often chosen by artists specifically for vertical and horizontal side panels of decorative ensembles. Examples of such treatment include the work of Giovanni Battista Tiepolo (fig. 28), Pierre Paul Prud'hon (fig. 29), and Denis. In addition, upon closer inspection, *Nude Woman* features a reduced schematic of rectangular forms at its base. Likewise, might the reduced schema at the base of *Nude Woman* be a distant echo of the plinth ubiquitous in sidebar figure compositions?

Picasso's entry into the realm of decorative painting could have been more directly inspired by Braque, whose family of decorator-painters was well-versed in the conventions of painted room interiors. In the winter of 1909 to 1910, Braque completed the pendant paintings *Piano and Mandola* and *Violin and Palette* (figs. 30, 31). Their vertical, oblong proportions indicate that he composed them with the decorative painting tradition in mind. Thus far scholars have not determined whether Braque executed them for a specific location or, as in the case of Renoir, they were painted without a secured commission in place. Equally undetermined is whether Braque knew of Picasso's meeting with Field and agreement to take on the commission.

Braque's choice of subject matter—the still life with musical instruments—was also typical for overdoor panels and may explain Picasso's next steps in the Field commission. Likely begun over the summer of 1911, which he spent in Céret, working in a studio provided to him by Frank Burty Haviland, *Pipe Rack and Still Life on a Table* (measuring 19½ by 50 inches, or 49.5 by 127 centimeters) and *Still Life on a Piano* (measuring 19¾ by 51¼ inches, or 50 by 130 centimeters) were completed in 1912 (pls. 12, 13). Despite differing degrees of finish, comparative visual analysis suggests that Picasso approached them as a pair. In Céret, Picasso enjoyed productive and fun-filled weeks in the company of his artist friends—Burty Haviland,

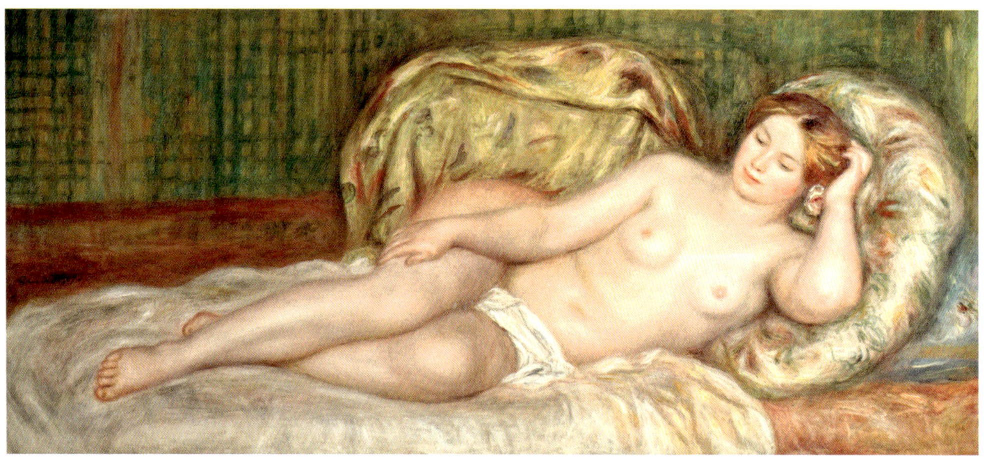

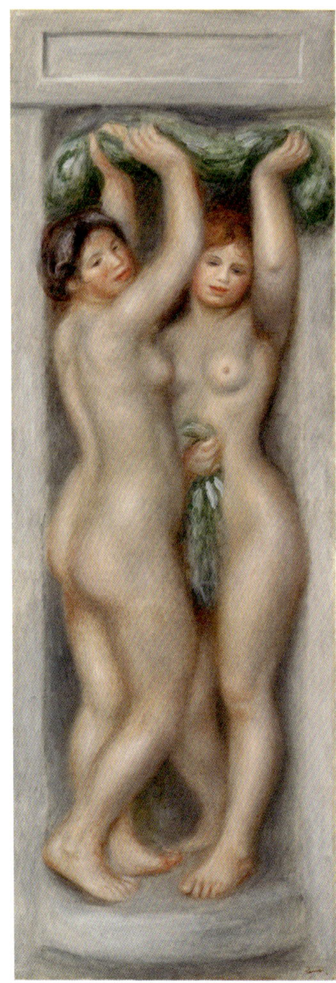

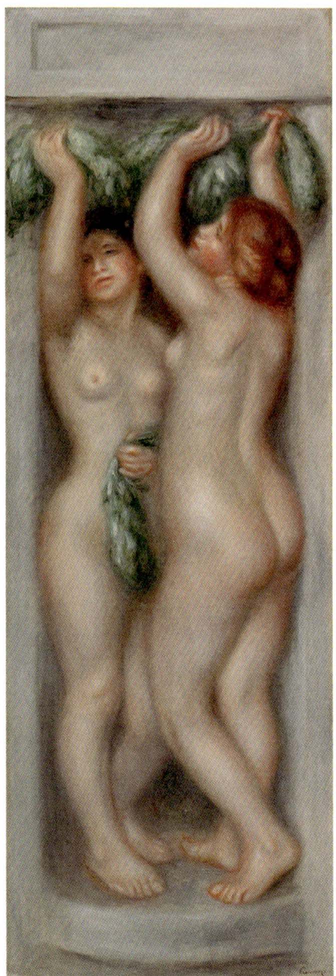

Fig. 25
Auguste Renoir, *Large Nude* (*Grand nu*), 1907. Oil on canvas, 28 × 61 ½ in. (71 × 156 cm). Musée d'Orsay, Paris, Donation par M. et Mme Robert Kahn-Sriber, en souvenir de M. et Mme Fernand Moch, 1975 (RF 1975 18)

Fig. 26
Auguste Renoir, *Caryatids* (*Cariatides*), also called *Deux baigneuses (panneau décoratif)*, ca. 1910. Oil on canvas, 51 ⅜ × 17 ⅞ in. (130.5 × 45.4. cm). Barnes Foundation, Philadelphia (BF918)

Fig. 27
Auguste Renoir, *Caryatids* (*Cariatides*), also called *Deux baigneuses (panneau décoratif)*, ca. 1910. Oil on canvas, 51 ⅜ × 17 ¾ in. (130.5 × 45.1 cm). Barnes Foundation, Philadelphia (BF919)

Fig. 28
Giovanni Battista Tiepolo and Girolamo Mengozzi (called Colonna), *Allegorical Figure Representing Grammar*, for the Palazzo Valle Marchesini Sala, Vicenza, Italy, 1760. Fresco, transferred to canvas, 146 × 57⅞ in. (370.8 × 147 cm). The Metropolitan Museum of Art, New York, Bequest of Grace Rainey Rogers, 1943 (43.85.16)

Fig. 29
Pierre Paul Prud'hon, *Evening* (*Le Soir*), an overdoor panel for the salon de la Richesse, Paris, 1798–1801. Oil on canvas, 28½ × 55½ in. (72.3 × 141 cm). Musée du Louvre, Paris (RF 2005 26)

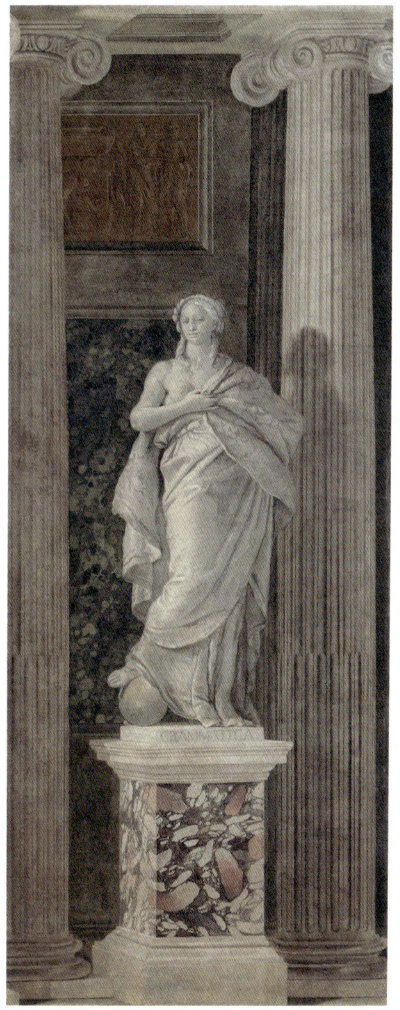

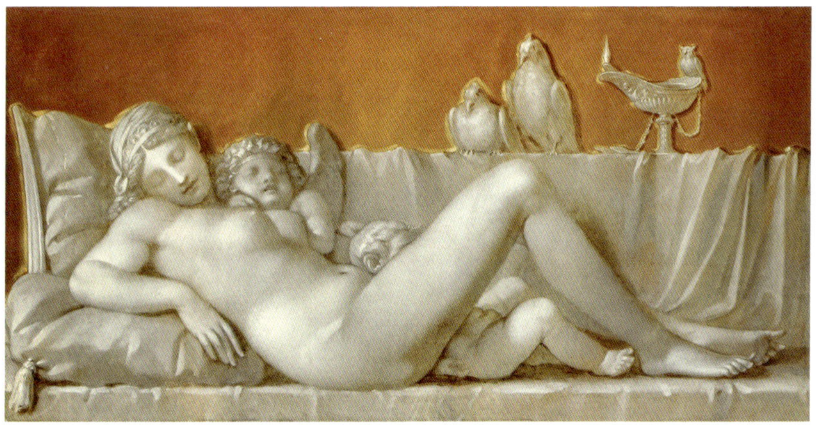

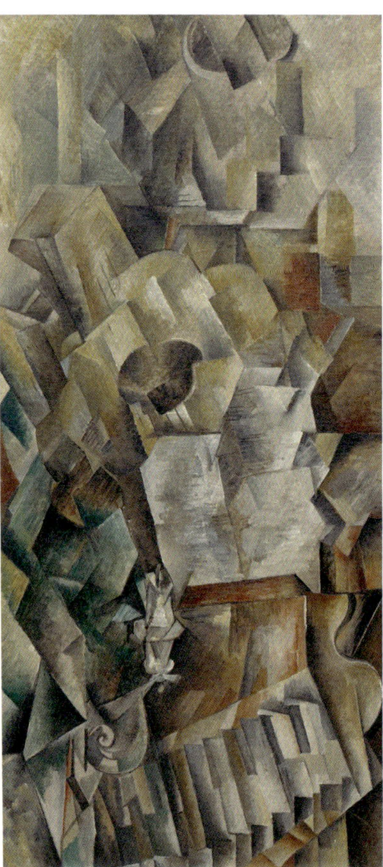

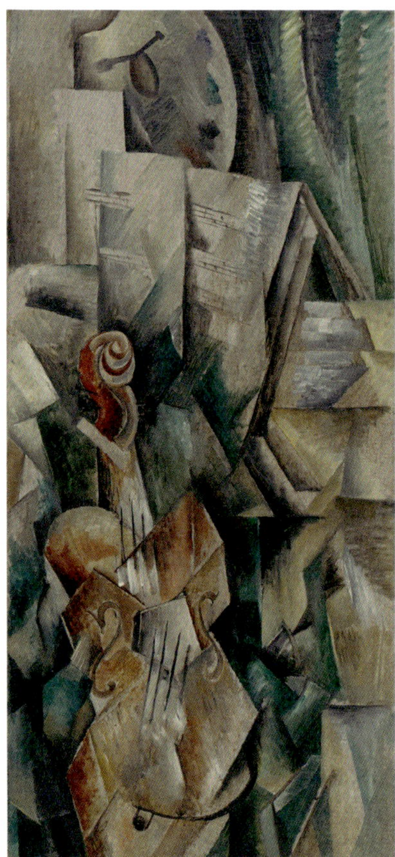

Manolo (Manuel Martínez Hugué), and Braque. The lively social atmosphere is reflected in these two still lifes, as well as in other works Braque and Picasso executed that summer. In addition to playing and listening to music, they enjoyed pipe smoking, alcohol drinking, card playing, and reading. For Picasso, the summer retreat from Paris concluded in late August when he returned to the French capital. Presumably, he brought the unfinished overdoor panels together with the rest of his Céret output, but the Field works would languish in his studio.

The evidence of the peripatetic early history of *Pipe Rack and Still Life on a Table* can be found on the work's surface and underlayers. The examination of the work by conservators at The Met, first Lucy Belloli and subsequently Isabelle Duvernois, revealed both the presence of oil paint from other wet paintings once stacked against it and scrapes and smears caused by objects touching its still-fresh surface.[83] These analyses also shed light on Picasso's creative process: the visible tack marks indicate that he attached

Fig. 30
Georges Braque, *Piano and Mandola*, 1909–10. Oil on canvas, 36 ⅛ × 16 ⅞ in. (91.7 × 42.8 cm). Solomon R. Guggenheim Museum, New York (54.1411)

Fig. 31
Georges Braque, *Violin and Palette*, 1909–10. Oil on canvas, 36 ⅛ × 16 ⅞ in. (91.7 × 42.8 cm). Solomon R. Guggenheim Museum, New York (54.1412)

the prepared canvas of fine weave to a wall. He used charcoal to delineate the outer edges of the composition, sketched the image out, and then employed an unusually wide range of paint consistencies, from washes to thick impasto. The composition is richly detailed at center with sizable left and right portions of the canvas left nearly empty. At the center, only a carafe, a cup, and a coffeepot's spout are readily identifiable, teasing the viewer's perception of reality and encouraging close examination of the work. A large transparent glass carafe just off-center in the painting is the most easily identifiable object, thanks to clearly delineated contours. While visually quiet, the sections at the far ends of the work nevertheless draw the viewer's attention. In these areas of the painting, Picasso used various pictorial devices not employed elsewhere in the commission. On the left-hand side he depicts a pipe rack fashioned from a piece of string held in place by a trompe l'oeil nail. The diagonal orientation of the painted string, in combination with the illusionistic nail, produces the effect of recessional pictorial space incongruous with the otherwise flat composition.

On the far right the viewer's eye is drawn to painted words and letters referencing printed matter, such as newspapers, books, pamphlets, and maybe even posters. Rendered in black paint is "Cc OCEAN"—a phrase that appears in two other Picasso paintings and the meaning of which is still unknown[84]—as well as the three letters "h e f," a possible allusion to Hamilton Easter Field, and "LA AUX DUMAS."[85] The latter refers to the nineteenth-century French classic *La dame aux camélias* (*The Lady of the Camellias*), published by Alexandre Dumas *fils* in 1848. The inclusion of the pipe rack points to a stereotypically male setting, and such makeshift holders are visible in photographs of both Picasso's and Braque's studios during this time, as well as in their paintings. The reference to Dumas's best-selling novel, however, opens the possibility of a more inclusive interpretation of the setting. *La dame aux camélias* centers around a female protagonist, and the book begins with a detailed description of her apartment, including her vanity table holding an extensive assortment of precious and beautiful objects. On June 23, 1912, in Avignon, Picasso attended a theatrical performance of the novel with Sarah Bernhardt in the title role.[86] Unfortunately, technical analysis of the panel cannot conclusively determine if Picasso added the Dumas reference around the time he saw the play or prior to it. Indeed, Picasso had already made his interest in French classic literature known by way of a Victor Hugo reference in a summer 1911 painting.[87]

Still Life on a Piano is richer and more darkly colored than its pendant, *Pipe Rack and Still Life on a Table*; however, its dense center and open ends echo those of its counterpart. With traces of the charcoal underdrawing still visible, it is in fact not much more legible than *Pipe Rack and Still Life on a Table*. Stacks of books and other reading material are replaced by musical instruments: a clarinet, violin, and piano. The instruments share the pictorial space with a hand fan, a stemmed glass, and a smoking pipe (the painting's descriptive title published by Christian Zervos in his catalogue raisonné is *Absinthe glass, bottle, fan, pipe, violin, and clarinet on a piano*), evoking an informal or private chamber music performance, not unlike those held in the Field residence in Brooklyn. The painting also recalls the lively summer in Céret. The faint "CER gran TES" (Céret Grand Fêtes / Great Feast / Celebration in Céret) on the left-hand side of the panel reinforces the work's musical theme, as do the hard black stencil letters "CORT"—a likely reference to the concert pianist Alfred Cortot.[88] Picasso added the stenciled letters—the first instance of the artist applying this technique in his work—after he saw his then close collaborator Braque use them in his painting (in late January 1911 at the earliest).[89]

Given that Picasso worked on the two still-life overdoors in tandem, one can surmise that he intended them to be installed in the library across from each other above the doors identified with the letters B and C in Field's floor plan. Thus, the bold stenciled and faint hand-painted word fragments in *Still Life on a Piano* would have played off the subtle word references in the opposite side of *Pipe Rack and Still Life on a Table*. Likewise, the rope-and-tassel passage on the far right side of *Still Life on a Piano* would have echoed the string of the pipe rack on the left in *Pipe Rack and Still Life on a Table*.

In the decorative painting tradition, these two still lifes align with the well-known motifs known as "the attributes." These images celebrate human creative and intellectual endeavors in the arts and sciences through the representation of objects associated with those pursuits, such as musical instruments. By adding such representations in his work, Picasso entered into a concurrent dialogue with Braque—who was the first Cubist to introduce musical instruments in his art—as well as one of his artist heroes, Jean Siméon Chardin. Picasso's two overdoor still lifes show similarities to Braque's pendant paintings mentioned above, *Piano and Mandola* and *Violin and Palette*, which could be read as attributes of music and the visual arts (see figs. 30, 31).[90] Furthermore, Braque's precedent offered a model for deploying Cubist pictorial strategies within the confines of a long and narrow space. Despite the obvious difference in orientation, some visual parallels emerge with Picasso's still-life overdoors for the Field library. A sequence of black-and-white piano keys appears along the bottom edge of both Braque's *Piano and Mandola* and Picasso's *Still Life on a Piano*, and both artists depict a curved sconce typically designed as a candleholder for pianos against a green background (the latter possibly referencing a cloth piano cover). In *Pipe Rack and Still Life on a Table*, Picasso also employed a trompe l'oeil nail, which in Braque's *Violin and Palette* holds up the artist's palette. In Picasso's painting, the nail holds up one end of the string that acts as the pipe rack. In both instances, the illusionistic nail and its cast shadow affirm the wall of the depicted room as well as the flatness of the picture plane.

Field's commission and Braque's pendant paintings likely would have prompted Picasso to look anew at two large Chardin still lifes in the Louvre collection, *The Attributes of the Arts* and *The Attributes of Music*, which Chardin painted as *dessus de porte* works for the royal château of Choisy, near Paris, in 1765 (figs. 32, 33). Removed from the chamber for which they were created, the panels eventually entered the Louvre's collection as autonomous easel paintings. Masterfully composed in a shallow space, each of Chardin's overdoors achieves balance and stability by focusing on a central object. In *The Attributes of the Arts*, the viewer's attention is drawn to the centrally situated tabletop plaster cast, the vertical orientation of which counters the overall horizontal orientation of the composition. In *The Attributes of Music*, the focus is the only large object placed horizontally within the still life—the mandolin. Comparable focal elements and orientation play are both found in the Picasso overdoor still-life panels. In *Pipe Rack and Still Life on a Table* Picasso adopted Chardin's compositional device of a centrally placed dominant vertical object, substituting Chardin's white plaster cast in *The Attributes of the Arts* with an anthropomorphized carafe. Furthering the link between the two paintings is the presence of the scroll or rolled papers, including their analogous placement within the respective compositions. Picasso's *Still Life on a Piano*, on the other hand, shares with Chardin's *Attributes of Music* not only its subject matter but also predominant overall horizontal thrust. Chardin's mandolin linking the composition's verticals is echoed in Picasso's panel by way of the hand fan, which performs a similar function.[91]

In his 1989 survey of the Field paintings, Rubin identified *Woman with a Guitar* of 1915 (pl. 14) and the reworked *Woman with a Fan* as the protracted endpoints of the artist's engagement with the commission (pl. 15). For Rubin, *Woman with a Guitar*—with its measurements of 72 ⅞ by 29 ⅝ inches, or 185 by 75 centimeters—was also a match for wall space H (though *Woman with a Fan* is a more likely one). It is tempting to connect *Woman with a Guitar* to the unaccounted-for oblong painting visible in the archival photograph of Picasso's studio at boulevard Raspail (see p. 38, fig. 21);

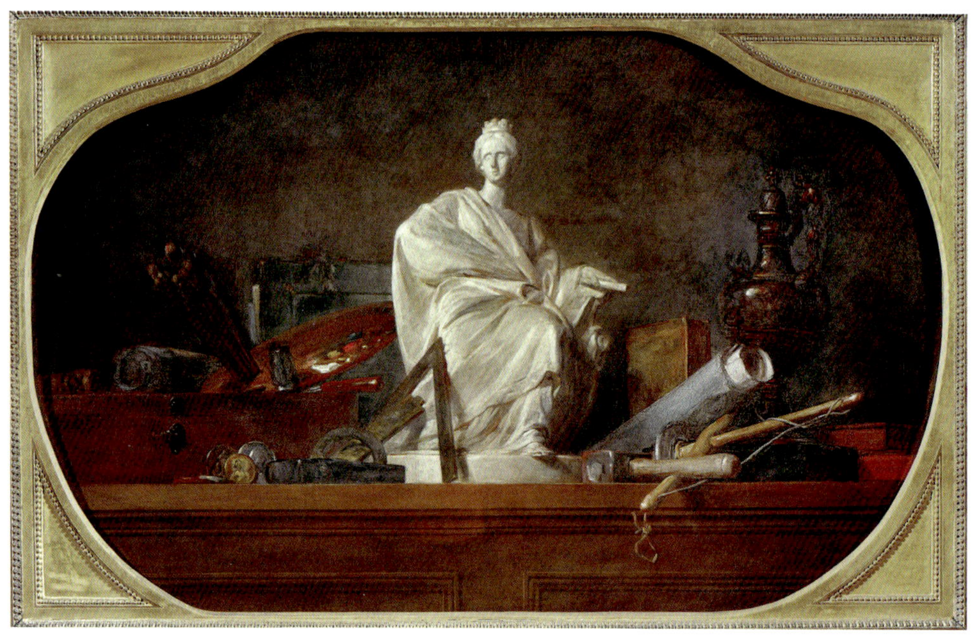

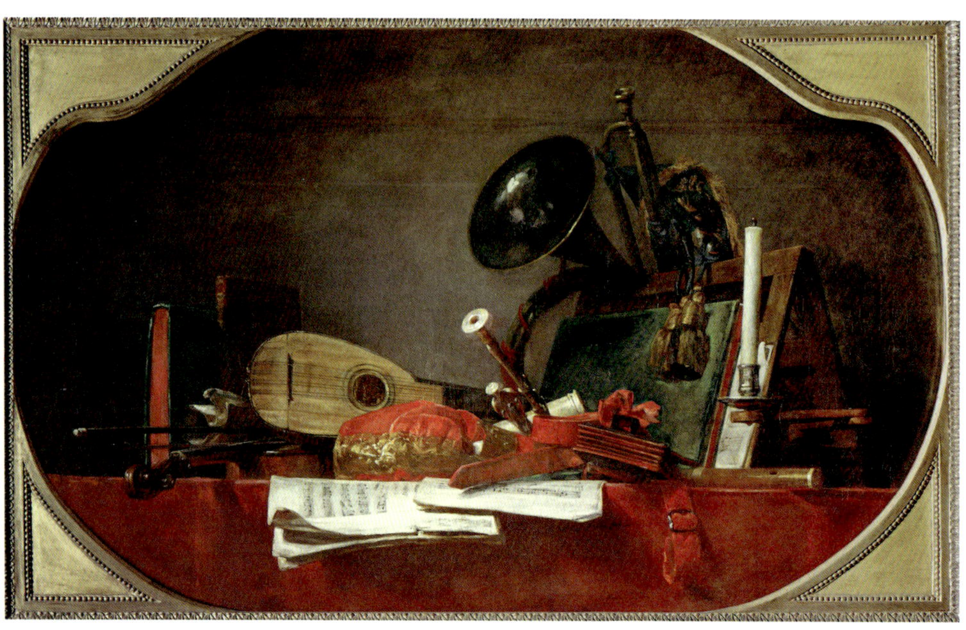

Fig. 32
Jean Siméon Chardin, *The Attributes of the Arts* (*Les Attributs des arts*), 1765. Oil on canvas, 35⅞ × 45⅜ in. (91 × 115 cm). Musée du Louvre, Paris (3199)

Fig. 33
Jean Siméon Chardin, *The Attributes of Music* (*Les Attributs de la musique*), 1765. Oil on canvas, 35⅞ × 45⅜ in. (91 × 115 cm). Musée du Louvre, Paris (3200)

however, nothing has yet been discovered to support this theory. Only scientific analysis of this painting (now in a private collection) may determine whether it resulted from a reprise of an earlier work or represents a completely new venture. With that said, also, there is at least one more painting in Picasso's oeuvre that fits the measurements of wall space H: *La Grecque* (1924; private collection).[92] Regardless, *Woman with a Guitar*, with its expansive color planes, array of textures, and inclusion of new iconography of the tailor's dummy head, is a dramatic change from the faceted forms, muted colors, and abstracted sign system of earlier Cubism. While continuing his engagement with the subject of the full-length musician, Picasso used the formal language of papiers collés and sheet-metal and cardboard constructions, which became a part of his Cubist practice in 1912, to make his paintings both more legible and abstract at the same time.

The same can be said about the revised *Woman with a Fan*, which Picasso altered in 1918 by adding a network of strong black contour lines and planes of flat blue and white color across the surface. In its new state, the painting brings to mind some figurative papiers collés or the large-scale painting *Harlequin and Woman with a Necklace* (1917; Musée National d'Art Moderne, Centre Georges Pompidou, Paris), which Picasso executed in Rome in spring 1917 while collaborating with the Ballets Russes on its production of *Parade*. The second layer of *Woman with a Fan*, superimposed over the 1910 composition, shows a sky-blue hue similar to that in the Rome picture, applied in an equally flat manner. Richardson provided possible circumstances that prompted Picasso to revisit *Woman with a Fan* in 1918. While the artist was abroad for the greater part of 1917, his studio—he resided in Montrouge, on the outskirts of Paris, as of October 1916—flooded, damaging some of its contents. The painting's new layer may have resulted from Picasso's desire to repair the water-damaged old composition.[93] The work, with its overlapping layers dating nearly eight years apart, acts as a record of the artist's collective experiments with large-scale decorative-format paintings and his lasting engagement with Field's commission.

PROMISING PANELS

Throughout the creation of all these works, there is no archival documentation that points to any communication between Field and Picasso past their exchange of letters in 1910. In the spring of 1911, Alfred Stieglitz, an

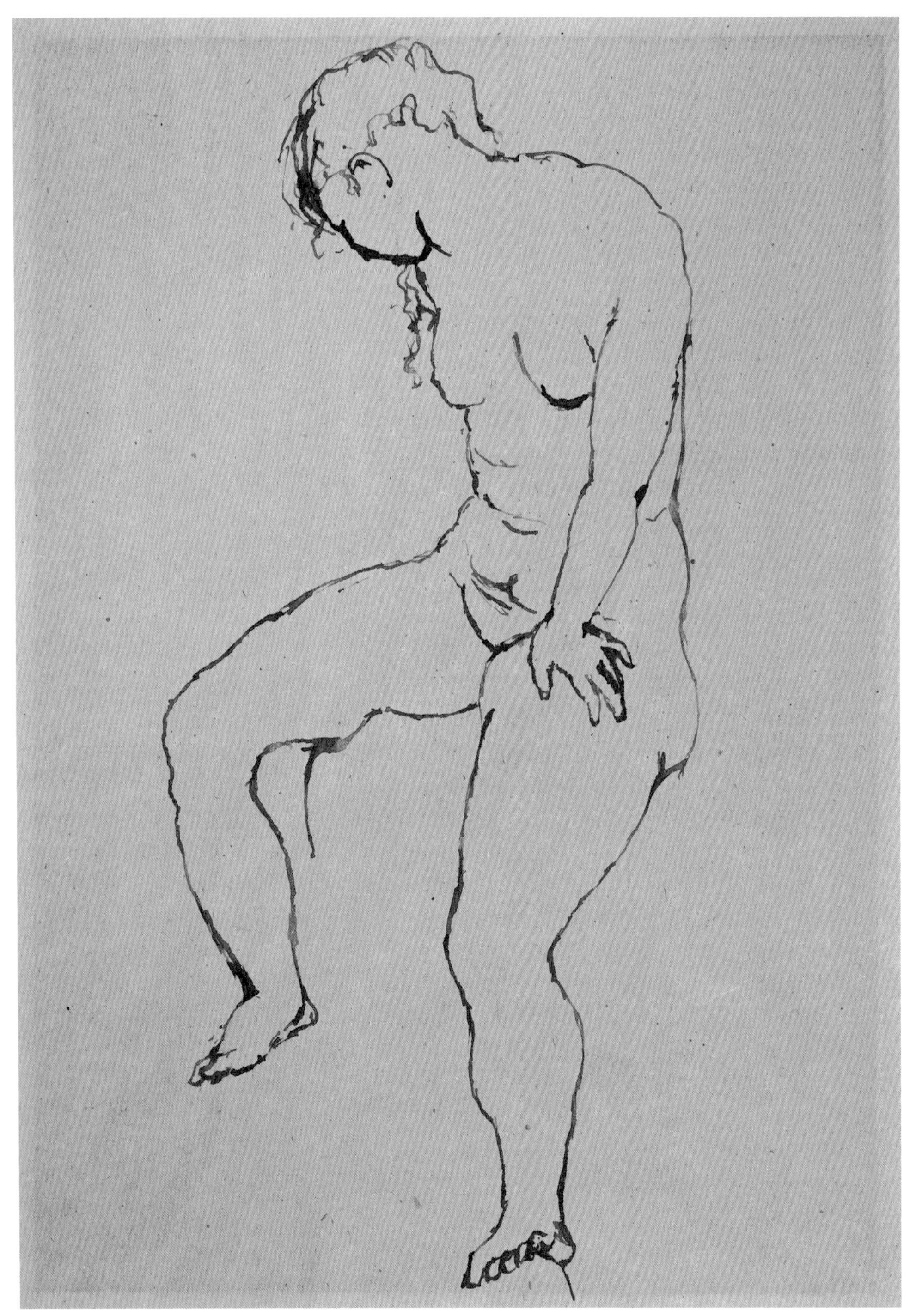

Fig. 34
Pablo Picasso, *Study of a Nude Woman*, ca. 1905–6. Pen and gray-brown ink on paper, 14 15⁄16 × 10 1⁄16 in. (38 × 25.6 cm). Museum of Fine Arts, Boston, John H. and Ernestine A. Payne Fund (1970.578)

acquaintance of Field and a friend of Paul Haviland (the latter also acted as Stieglitz's financial backer), hosted at his gallery 291 the first Picasso exhibition in the United States. By Stieglitz's own account, Field made repeated journeys to Manhattan to view the selection of eighty-three drawings, and other than Stieglitz himself, was also the sole buyer.[94] Both Americans selected works of the same subject matter, a female nude, but while Stieglitz went for a recent work, the refined Cubist charcoal composition *Standing Female Nude* (pl. 7), Field opted for an earlier and more conventional pen-and-ink *Study of a Nude Woman* from around 1906 (fig. 34). It was his first acquisition of the artist's work. Later that year, in the early fall, Stieglitz traveled to Paris, where he met Picasso for the first time. He likely told the artist about Field's purchase and in turn was shown some of the panels. According to Laurent's recollection, Field, in fact, had asked Stieglitz to check on Picasso's progress on his commission.[95] Upon his return, Stieglitz reached out to Field to finalize the purchase of the drawing and used the occasion to report: "In Paris I saw your panels started. They promise much."[96] In reply, Field praised the drawing he had acquired, but, curiously, left Stieglitz's comment about the panels unacknowledged.[97] (For reproductions of these letters, see p. 94.) Field's silence or inaction cannot be attributed to a changed opinion of Picasso but perhaps to his initial intent to keep the public knowledge of the commission under wraps. The following year, on the occasion of Field's solo exhibition of his paintings at the American branch of the Berlin Photographic Company, managed by dealer Martin Birnbaum, Field wrote admiringly of Picasso and discussed the impact of the Spaniard in the catalogue foreword: "Since my return to America I have been most influenced, perhaps, by four hard workers, Arthur [B.] Davies, Picasso, Maurice Sterne, and [Sir William] Rothenstein. It is perhaps misleading to speak of these men as having influenced me. They have rather given me the courage to be true to myself."[98] Years later, in May 1919, Field delivered his most emphatic acknowledgment of his high regard for Picasso in the pages of the *Brooklyn Daily Eagle*. He was an "isolated genius" whom Field ranked "as one of the greatest living artists, one of the men of our time who will be admired a century hence."[99]

While consistently open about his high esteem for Picasso's art, initially, Field was publicly less forthcoming about the commission. The art critic Henry McBride, one of Field's acquaintances and a visitor to 106 Columbia Heights, recalled being told by Field about the commission in confidence. According to McBride, Field explained that he did not intend to install the panels while his mother was alive so as to avoid subjecting her to living with Picasso's Cubism, or as McBride put it, "such extraordinary work."[100] While this explanation is plausible, it is impossible to determine the role Lydia Haviland Field's artistic sensibility played in her son's hands-off attitude toward the commission. McBride's characterization of Mrs. Field as supportive of her son's activities and open to new forms of artistic expression casts doubt that her disapproval was the primary reason.[101]

At last, Field made the public reveal of the commission in the aforementioned November 1919 *Brooklyn Daily Eagle* art column, two years after his mother's death.[102] There, Field not only recounted the circumstances of when and how the commission came about but also admitted that "the decorations are not yet finished."[103] In this statement, Field comes across as a facilitator who is content to provide a fellow artist with a platform (or, in this case, walls of a home library) from which to investigate his own practice. Perhaps he was also still excited by having convinced Picasso to take on his first commission for a decorative ensemble. Certainly, Field does not give the impression of being discouraged or disappointed by the delay. Since the project was agreed upon, Picasso's painting, in Field's opinion, "has become more suited to wall decoration, more in harmony with stone, plaster, cement. His line, his masses have gained in delicacy without losing force."[104] Field's description conjures Picasso's early Cubism, with its restricted palette of browns, ochers, yellows, and grays, and textures ranging from light washes to rich impasto of works like *Nude Woman* or *Reclining Woman on a Sofa*. While no longer traveling to Europe on a regular basis due to his increased involvement with the local American modern art scene,[105] and then hindered by the outbreak of World War I, Field had opportunities to follow Picasso's artistic progression from Brooklyn, both through publications and in commercial art galleries across the East River, such as Carroll Galleries, Modern Gallery, and Washington Square Gallery—all of which displayed Picasso's paintings and works on paper, Cubist and otherwise, in their exhibitions prior to the war.[106] The 1913 Armory Show—Field attended the opening reception and visited it multiple times—would have been another opportunity to encounter Picasso's Cubist painting. However, it appears that in late 1919 Field was not up to date on the Spaniard's latest Cubist imagery—by then characterized by strong colors and unmodeled planes—or chose to ignore it.[107]

Field's best opportunity to follow up with Picasso was when he finally returned to Europe in 1920, journeying across the Continent in June and July.[108] It is possible that Field obtained an update on his panels when he passed through Paris. According to Laurent, he and Field at some point in time learned that Picasso had "sold the paintings for a much higher price to a Russian collector."[109] He also added that Field did nothing about it. Laurent failed to disclose the source of this rumor. Did it perhaps originate with Picasso, who did not wish to revisit the project? For this reason and because there is no record of Picasso's ever discussing the commission with anybody, it is easy to dismiss the project as inconsequential to his practice and to continue to consider the works he executed for it as stand-alone easel paintings, albeit of odd proportions. Yet, it is difficult to ignore the extraordinary amount of sustained energy that Picasso devoted to the commission without any pressure from Field. Contrary to Laurent's statement, the canvases stayed with the artist long after Field's death in 1922. Two paintings, *Man with a Guitar* and *Man with a Mandolin*, never left his possession. Rather, Picasso treated the commission, and the challenges of the architectural space for which it was created, as an open-ended investigation of his continuously changing Cubist practice and an opportunity to engage with the decorative painting tradition.

PLATES

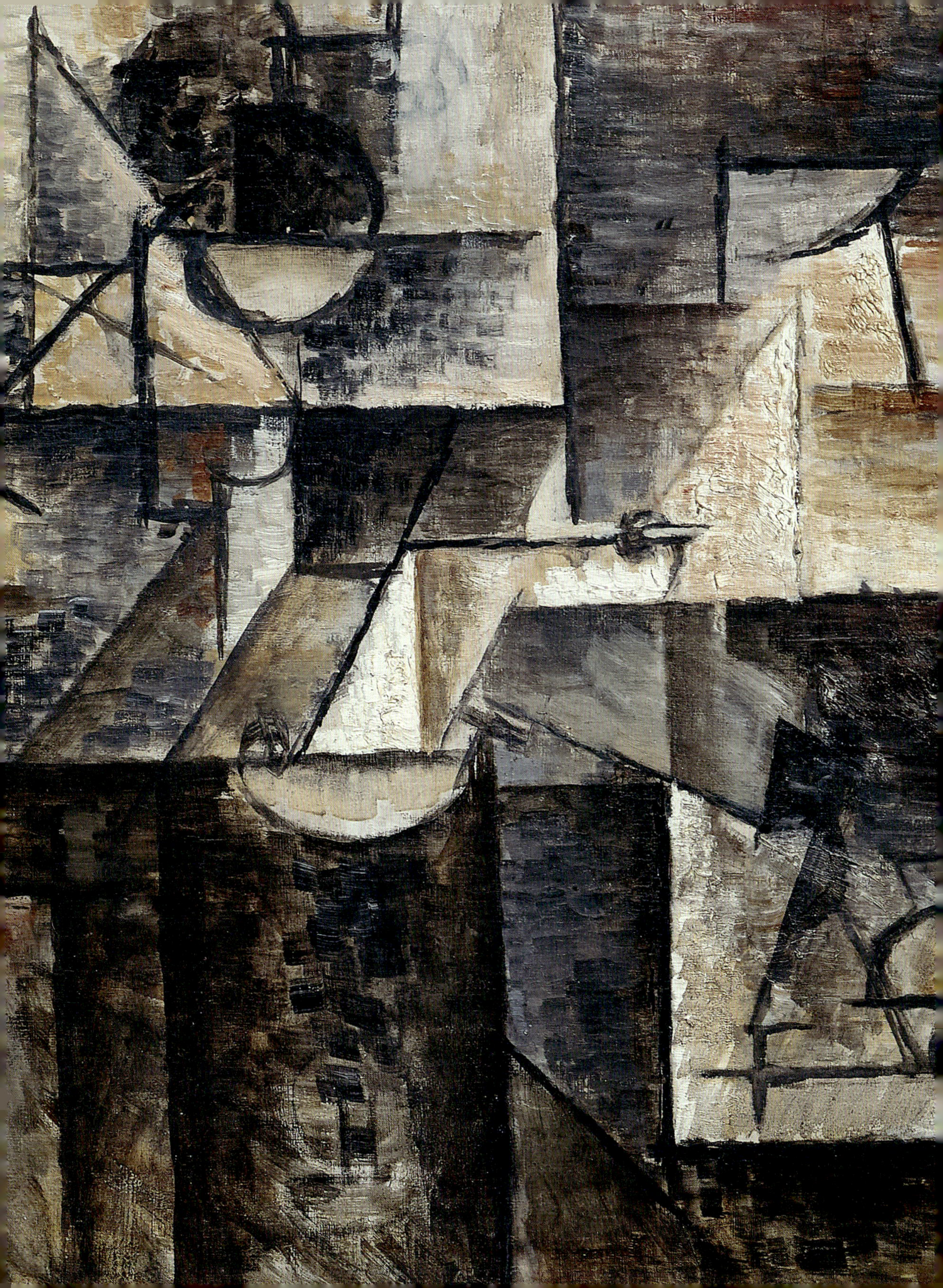

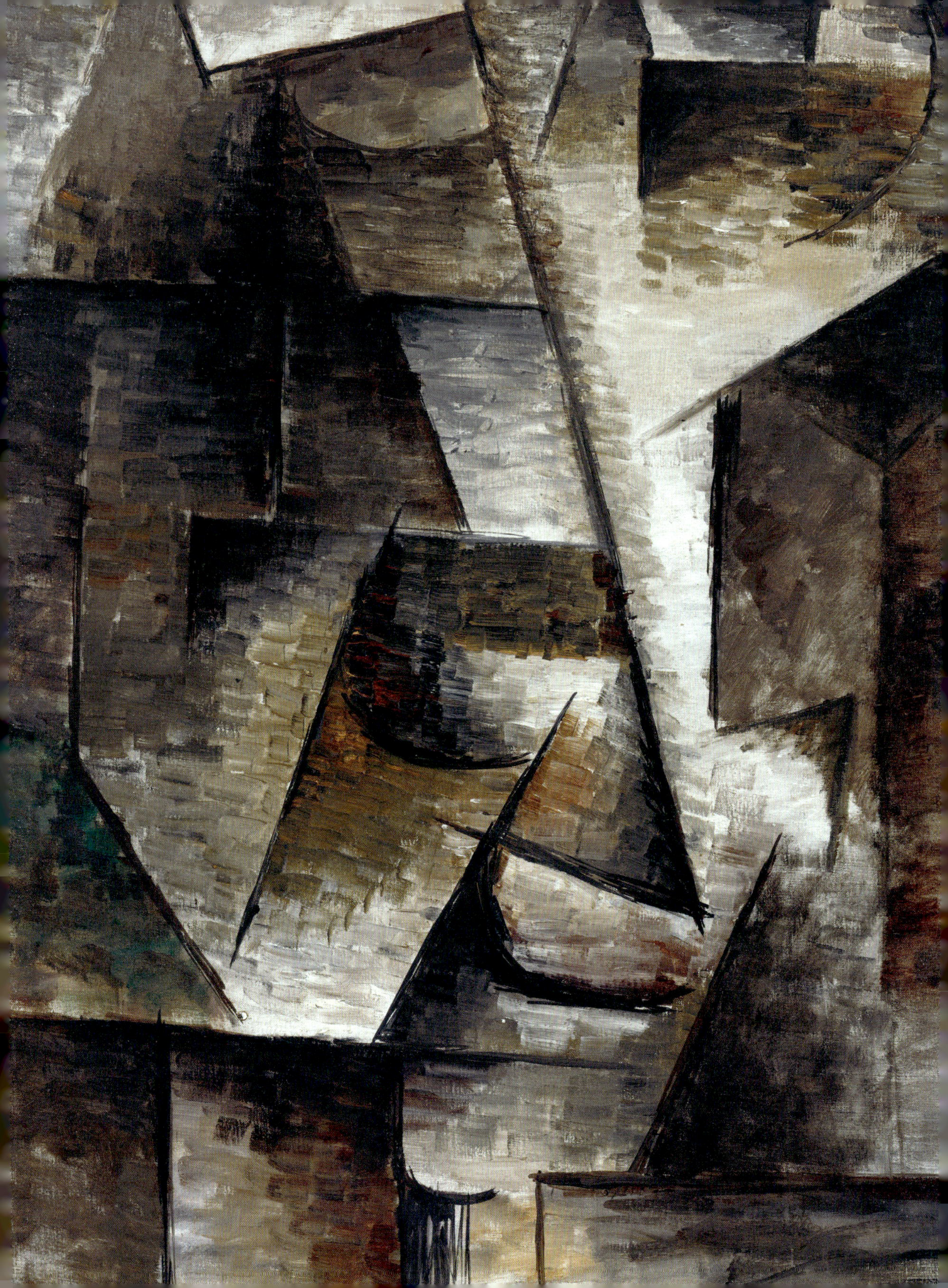

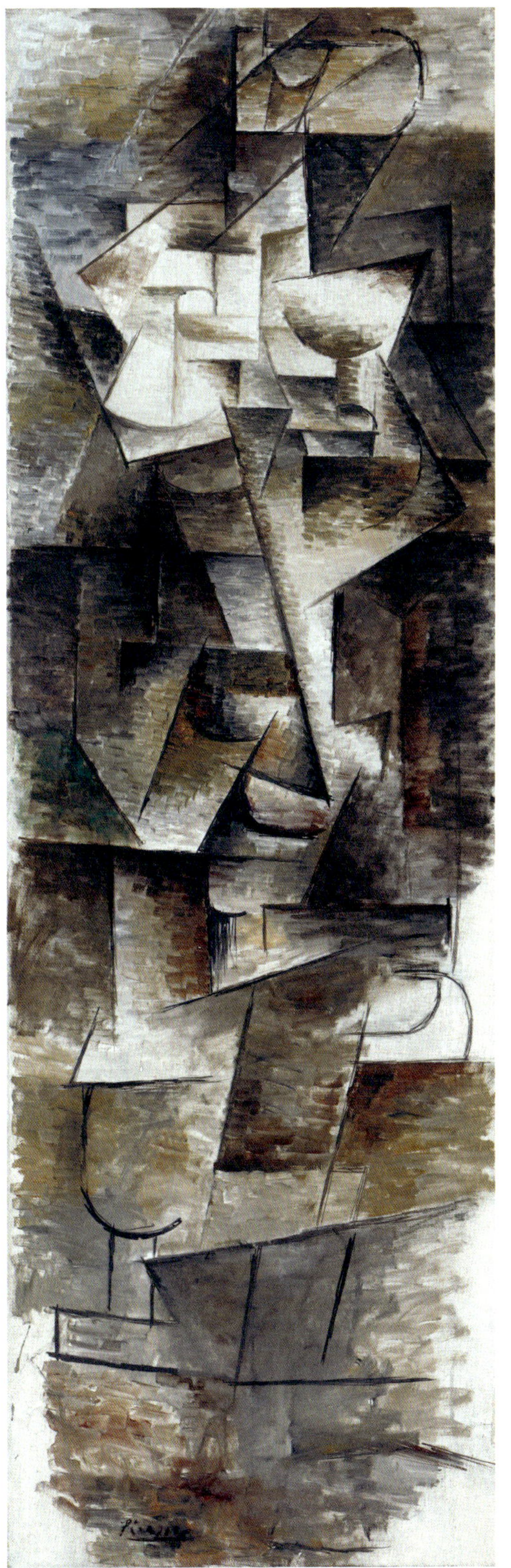

Plate 1
Nude Woman, summer or fall 1910

Plate 2
Female Nude,
spring 1910

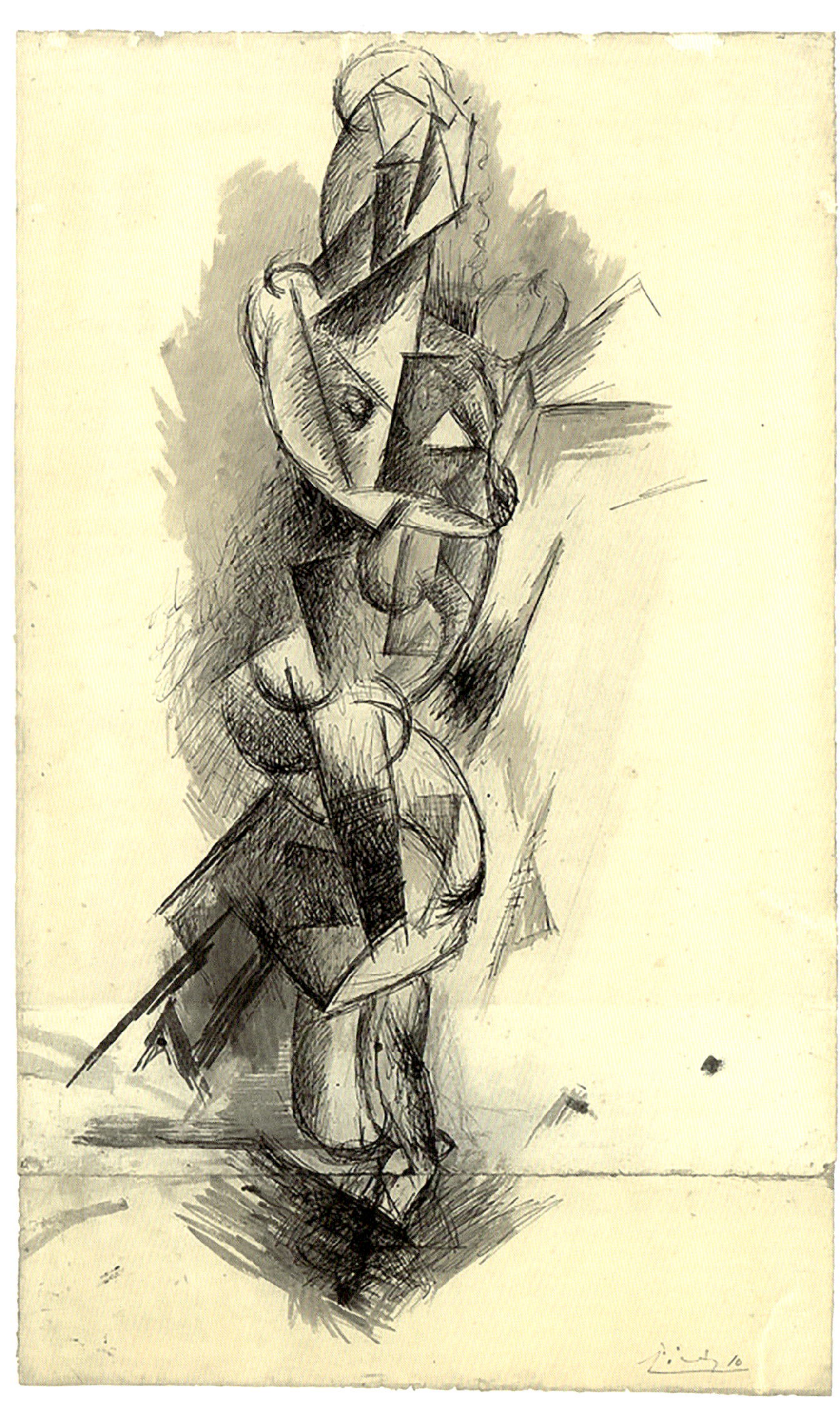

Plate 3
Standing Nude,
summer 1910

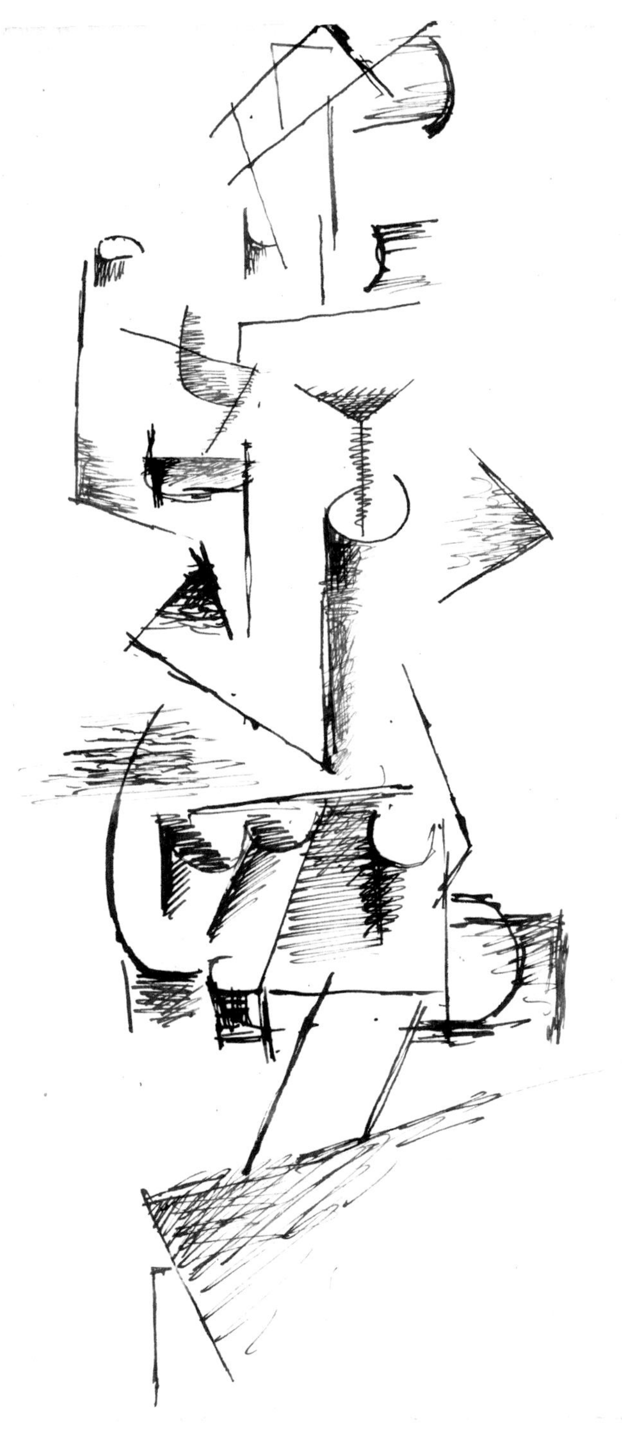

Plate 4
Standing Female Nude,
summer 1910

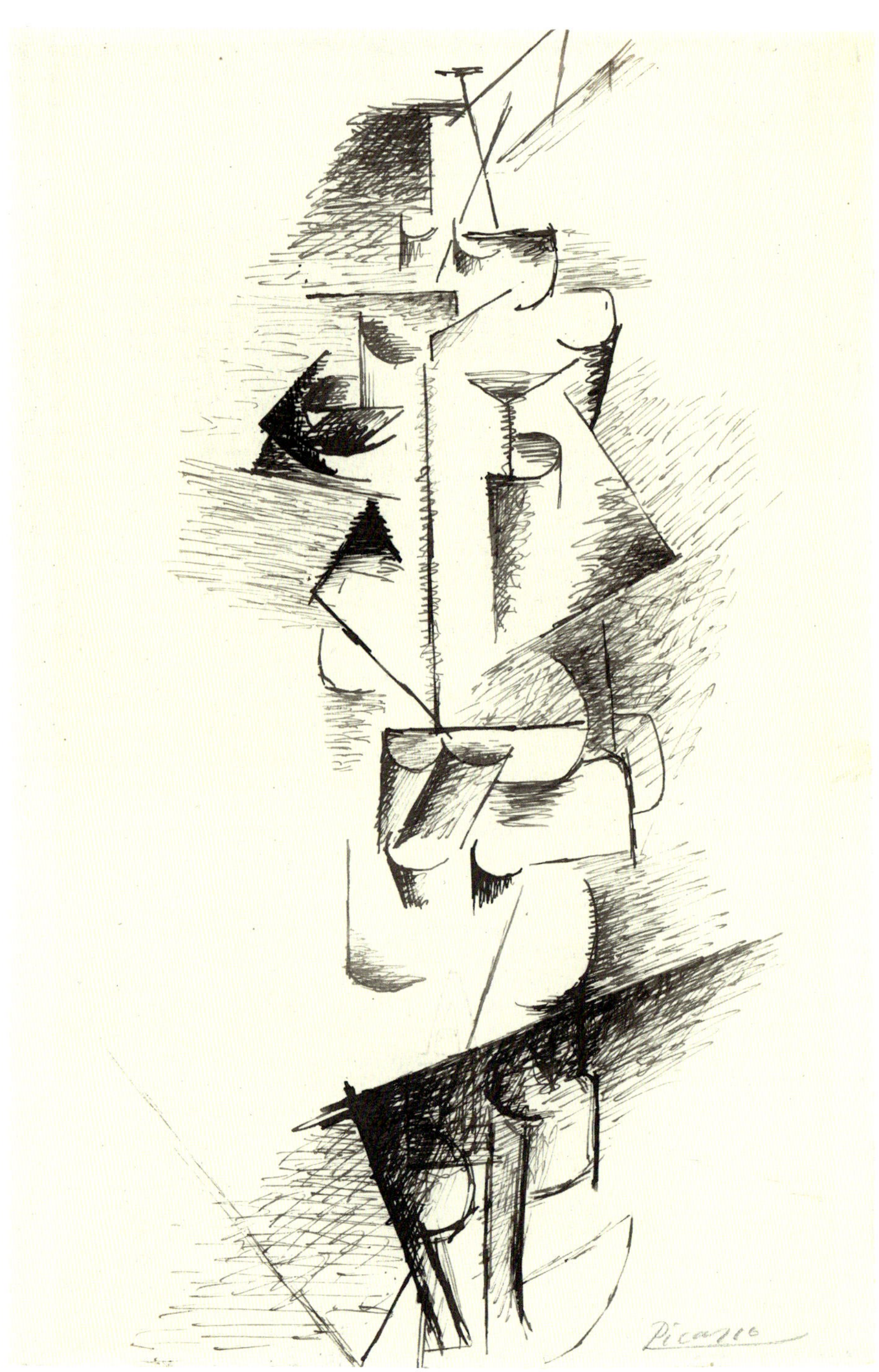

Plate 5
Nude, summer 1910

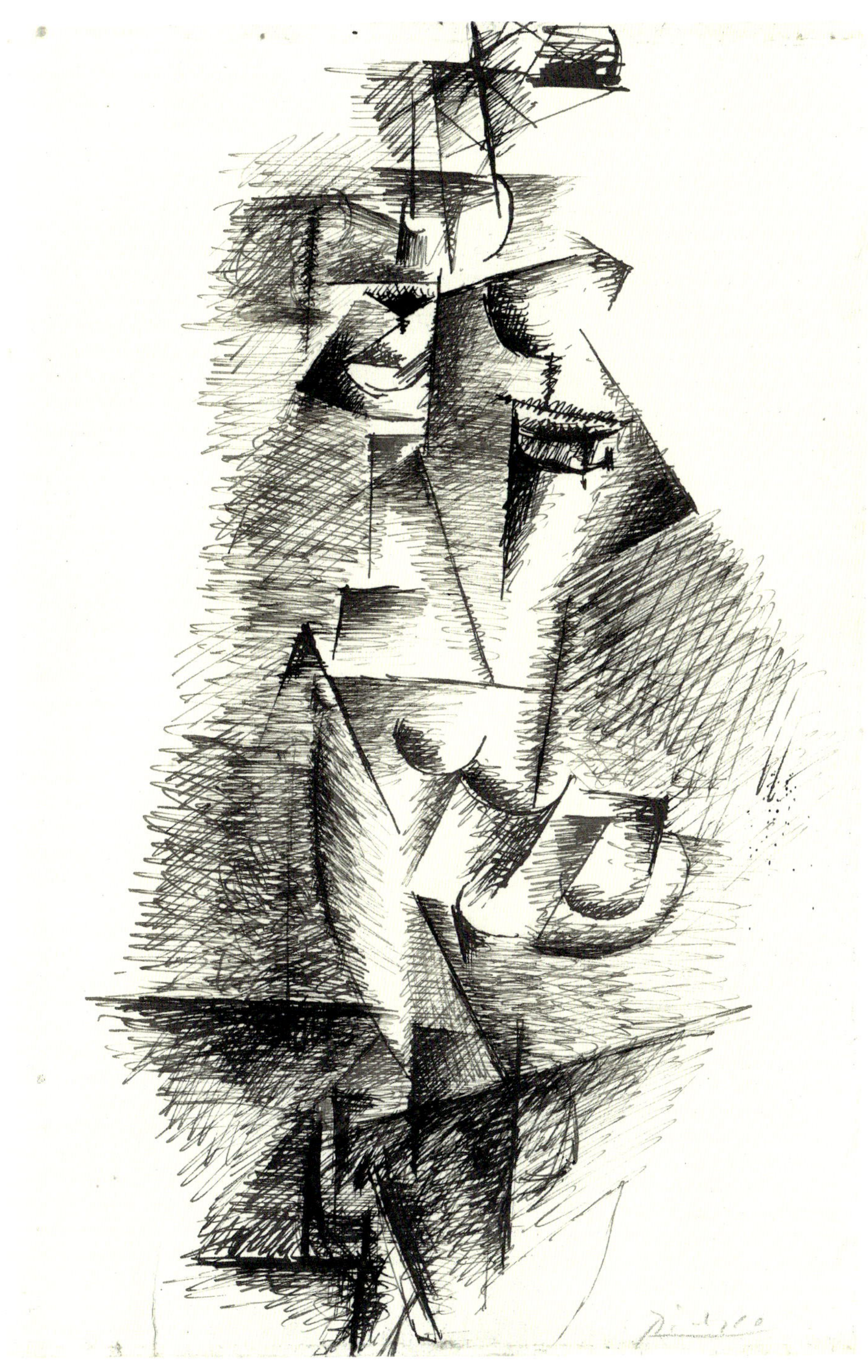

Plate 6
Standing Nude Woman,
summer or fall 1910

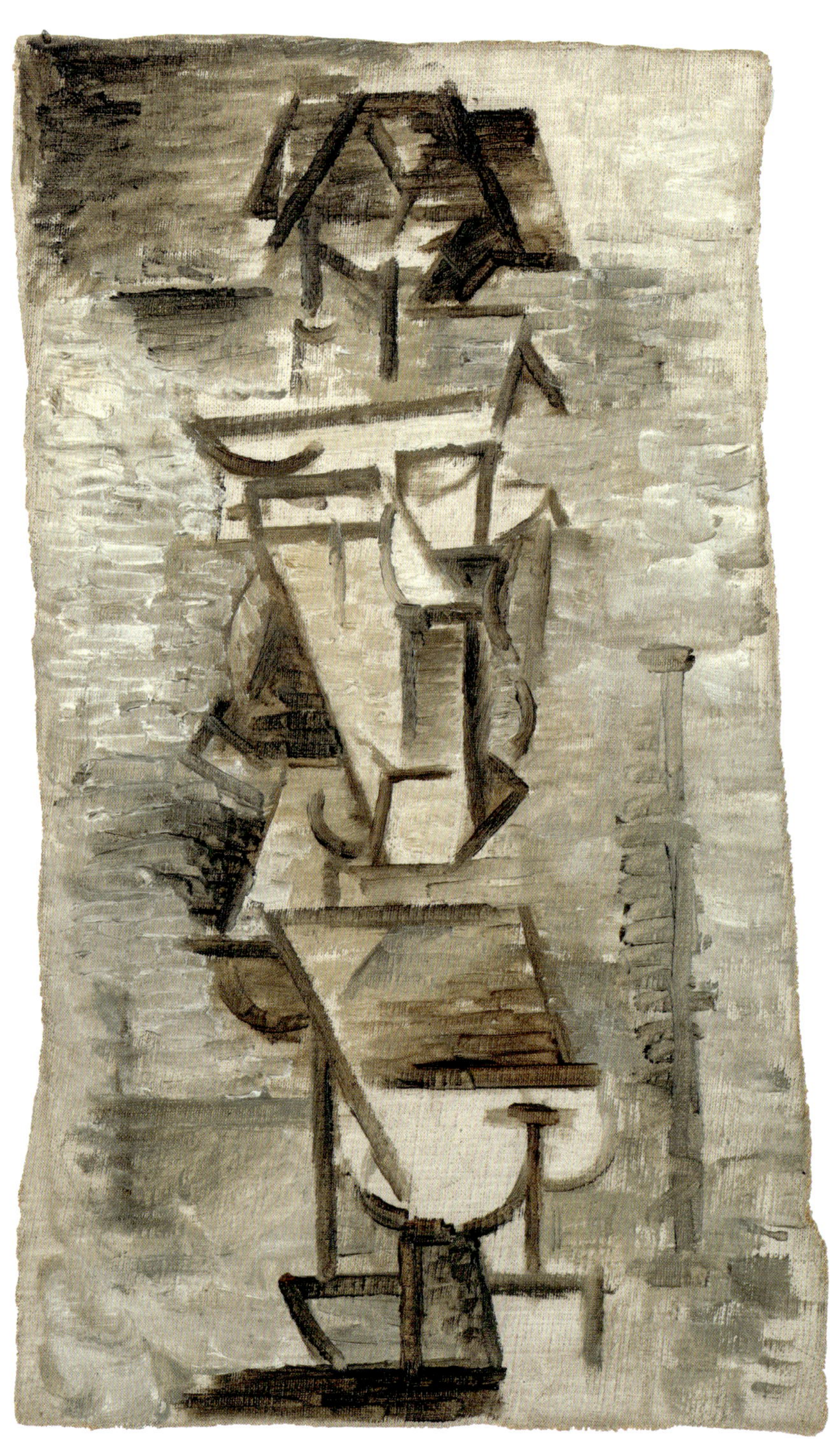

Plate 7
Standing Female Nude,
fall 1910

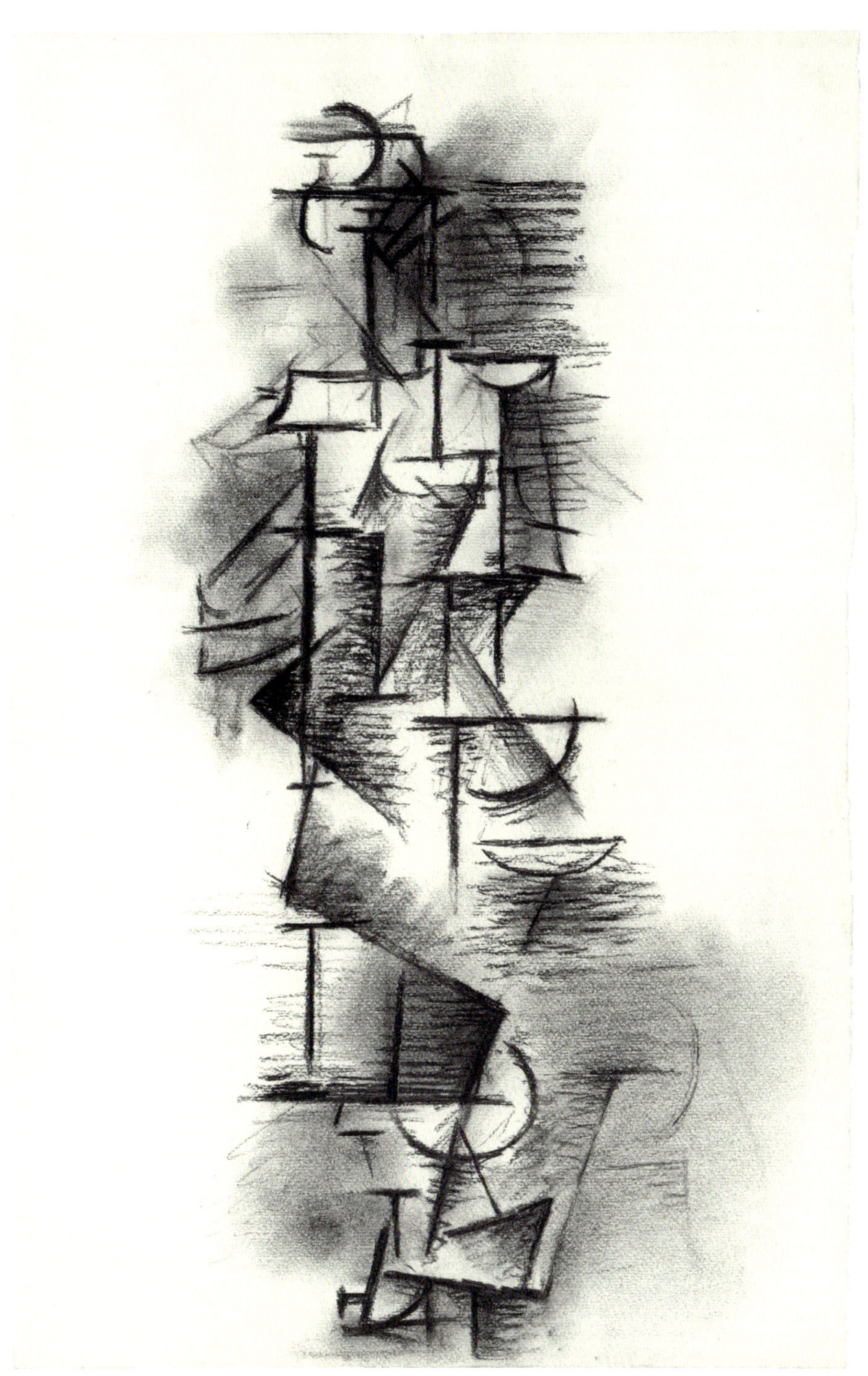

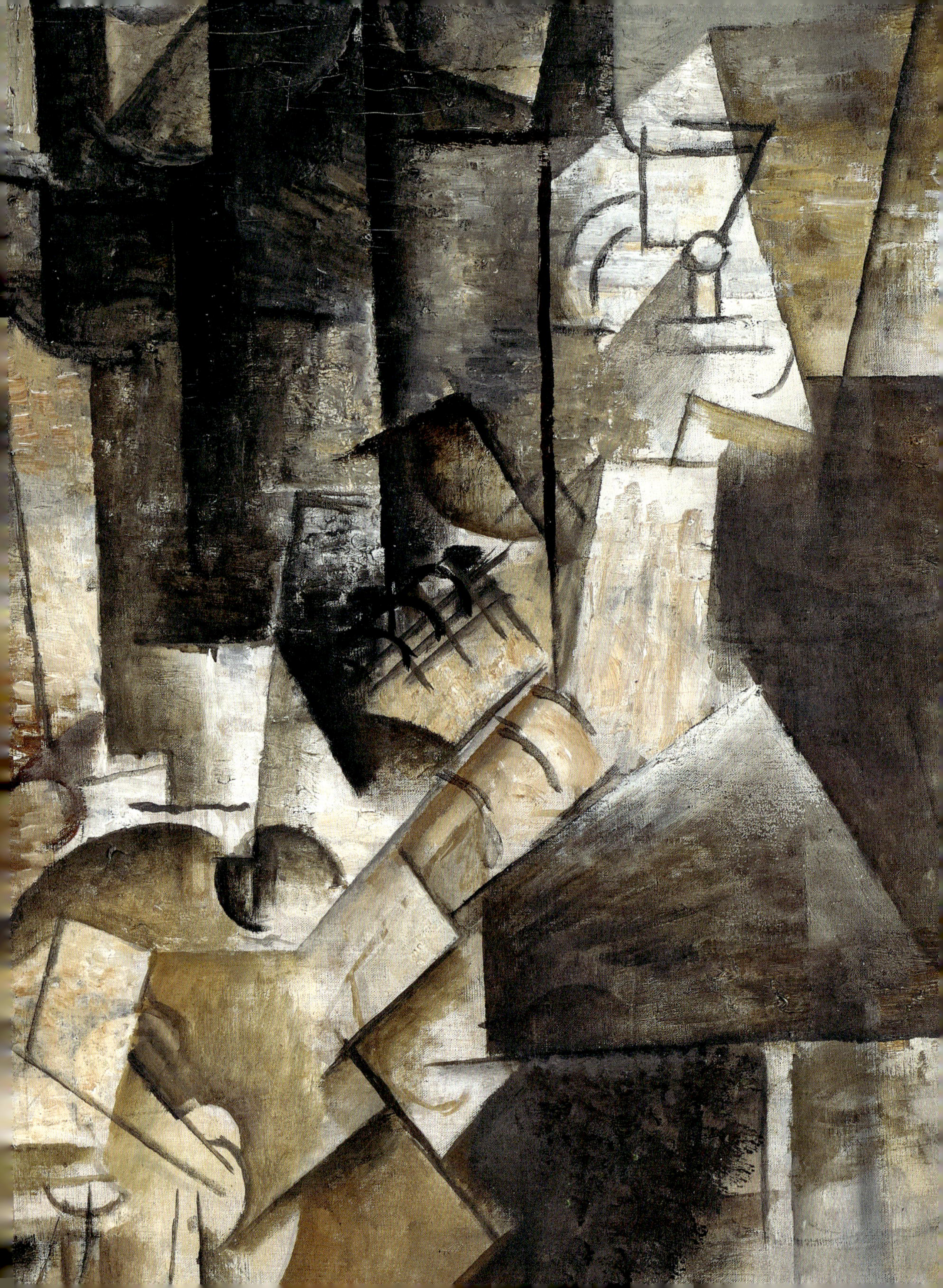

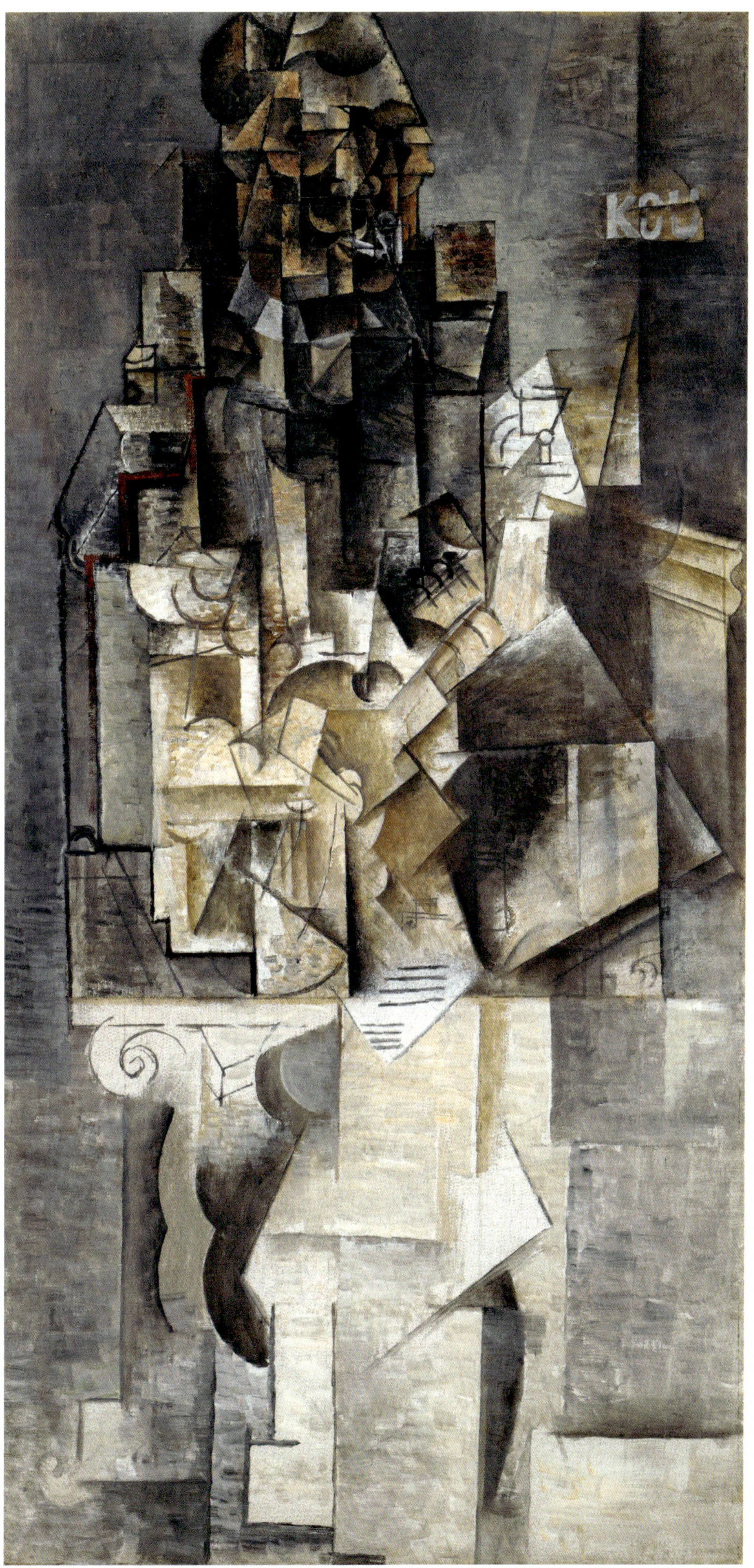

Plate 8
Man with a Guitar, summer/fall 1911, reworked in 1913

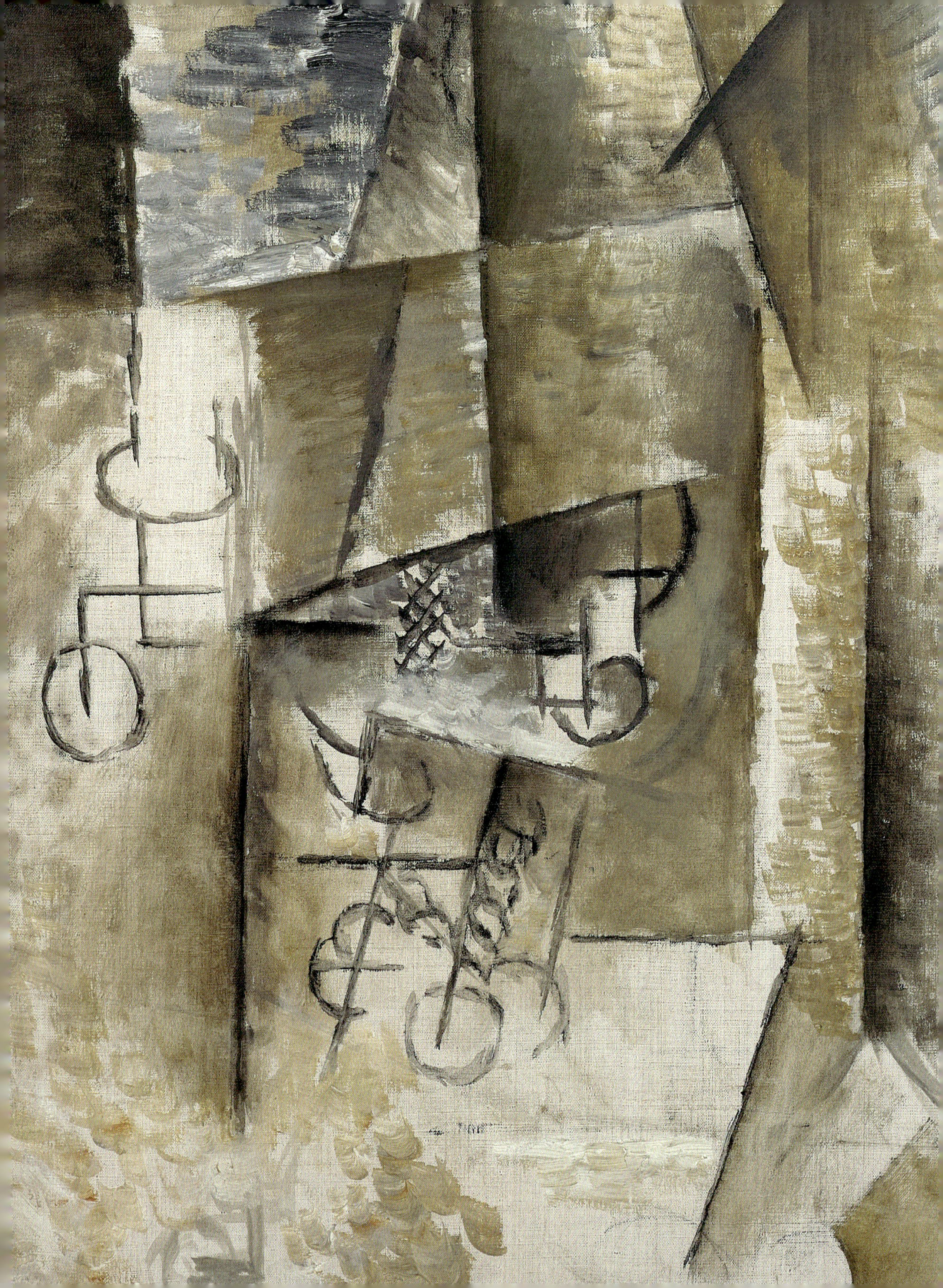

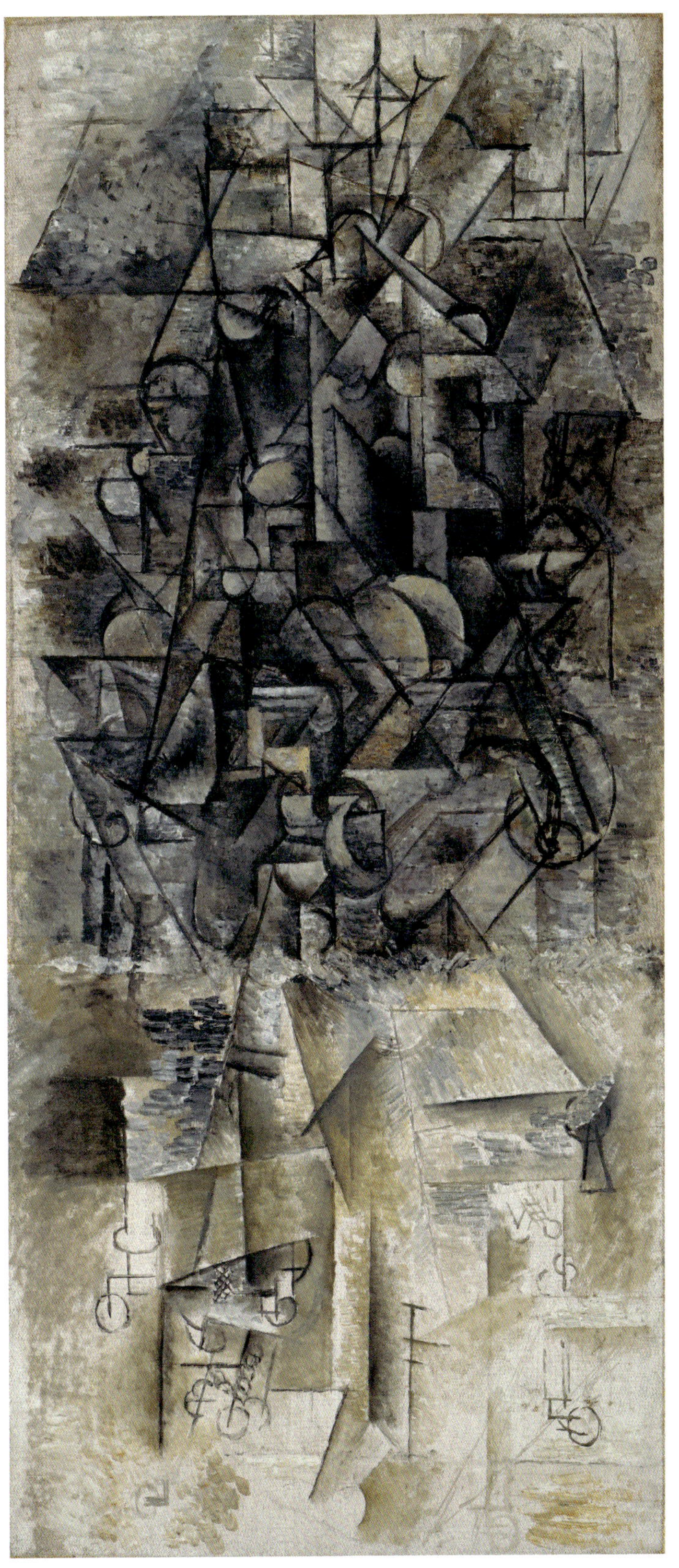

Plate 9
Man with a Mandolin, summer/fall 1911

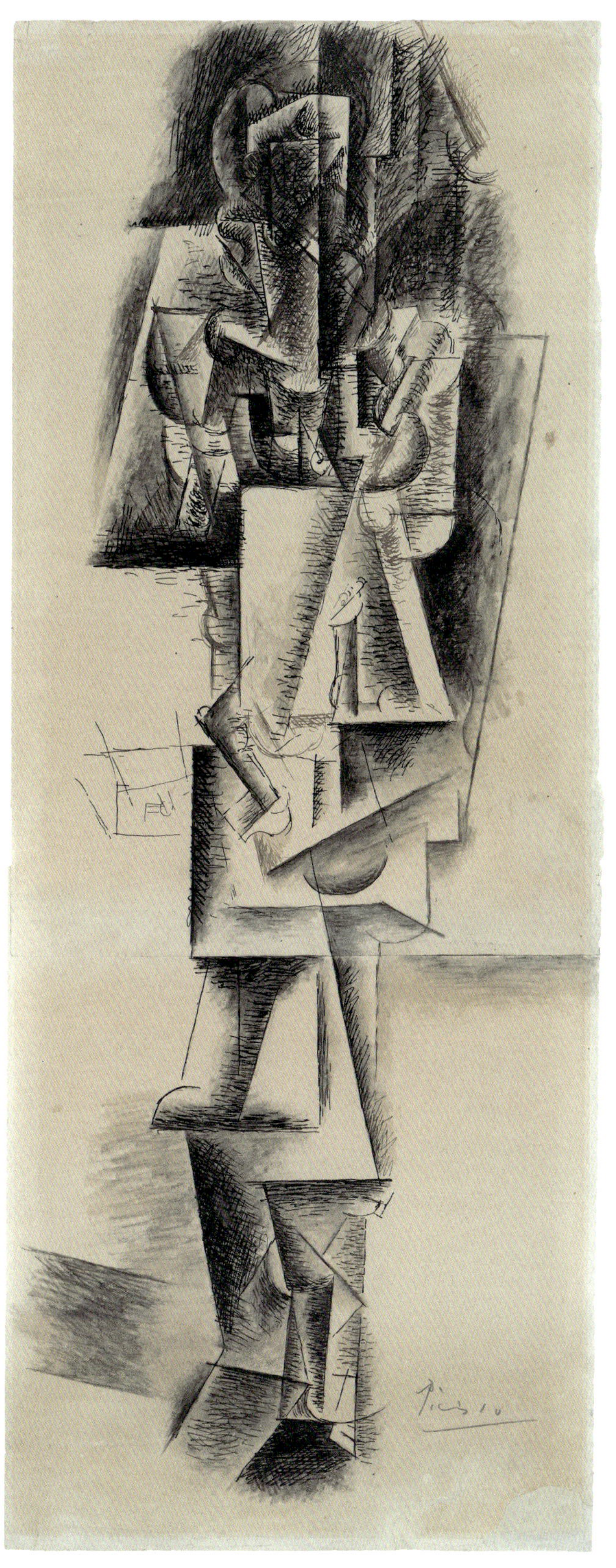

Plate 10
Standing Woman,
summer 1912

Plate 11
Reclining Woman on a Sofa, fall 1910

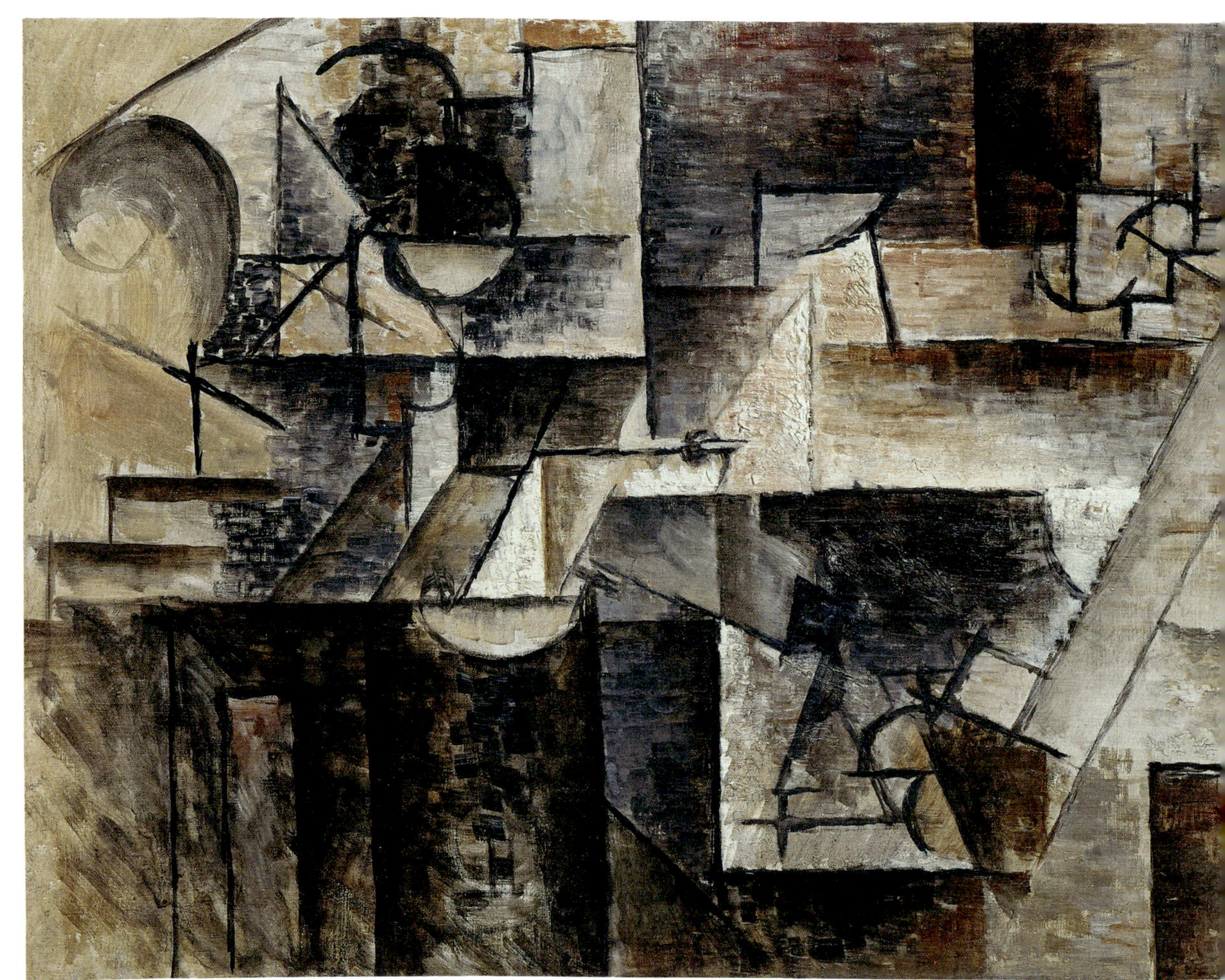

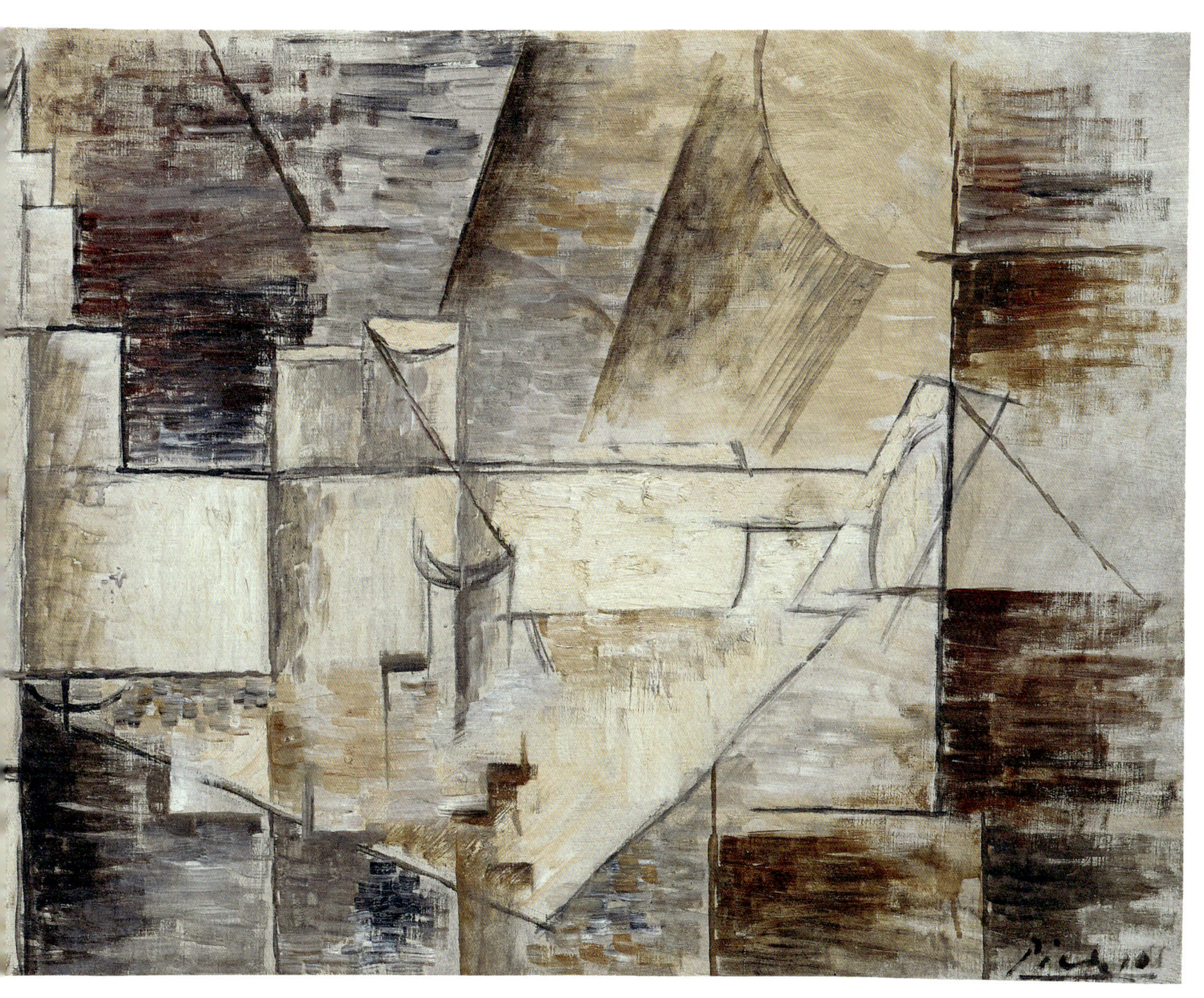

Plate 12
Pipe Rack and Still Life on a Table, summer 1911

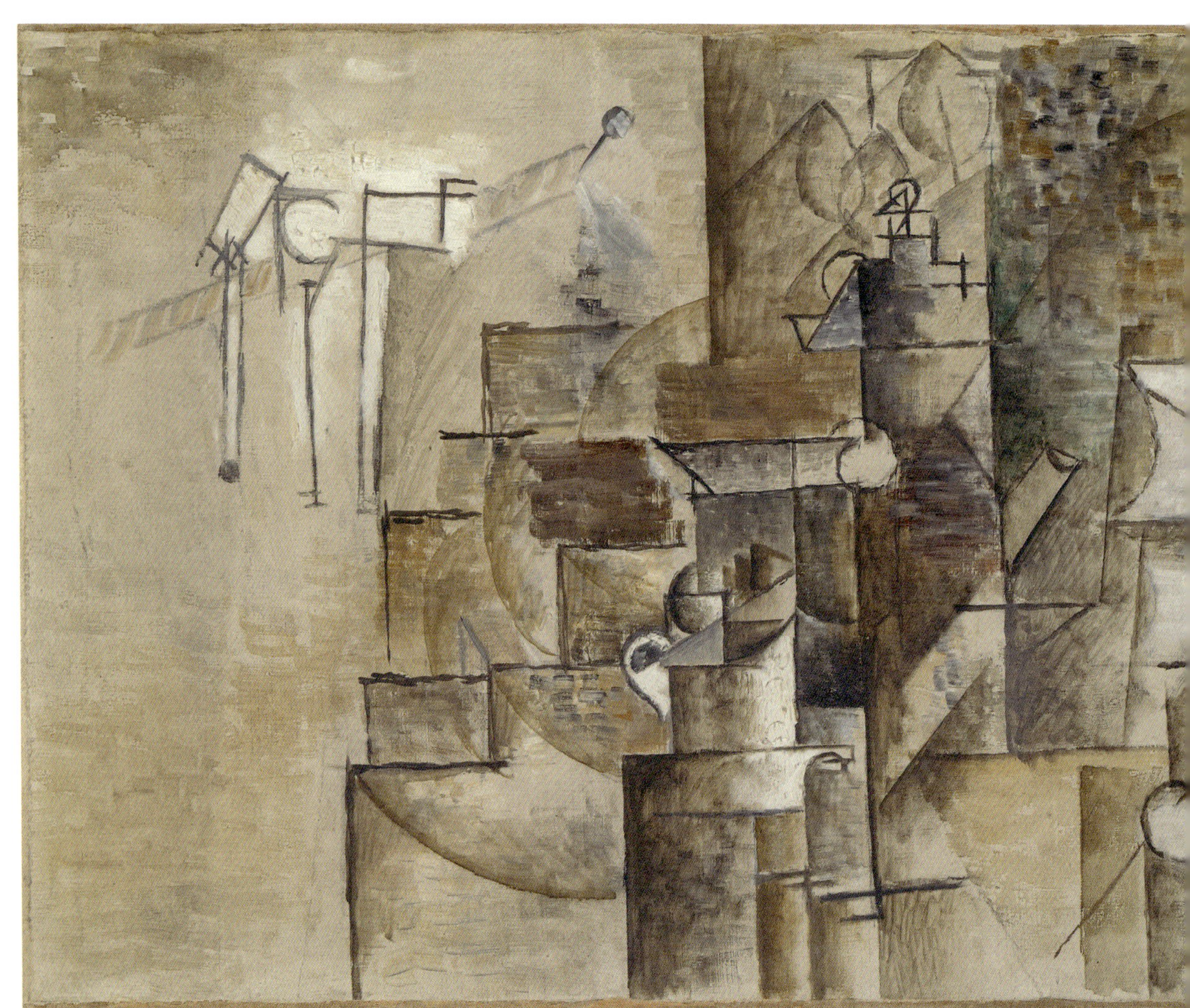

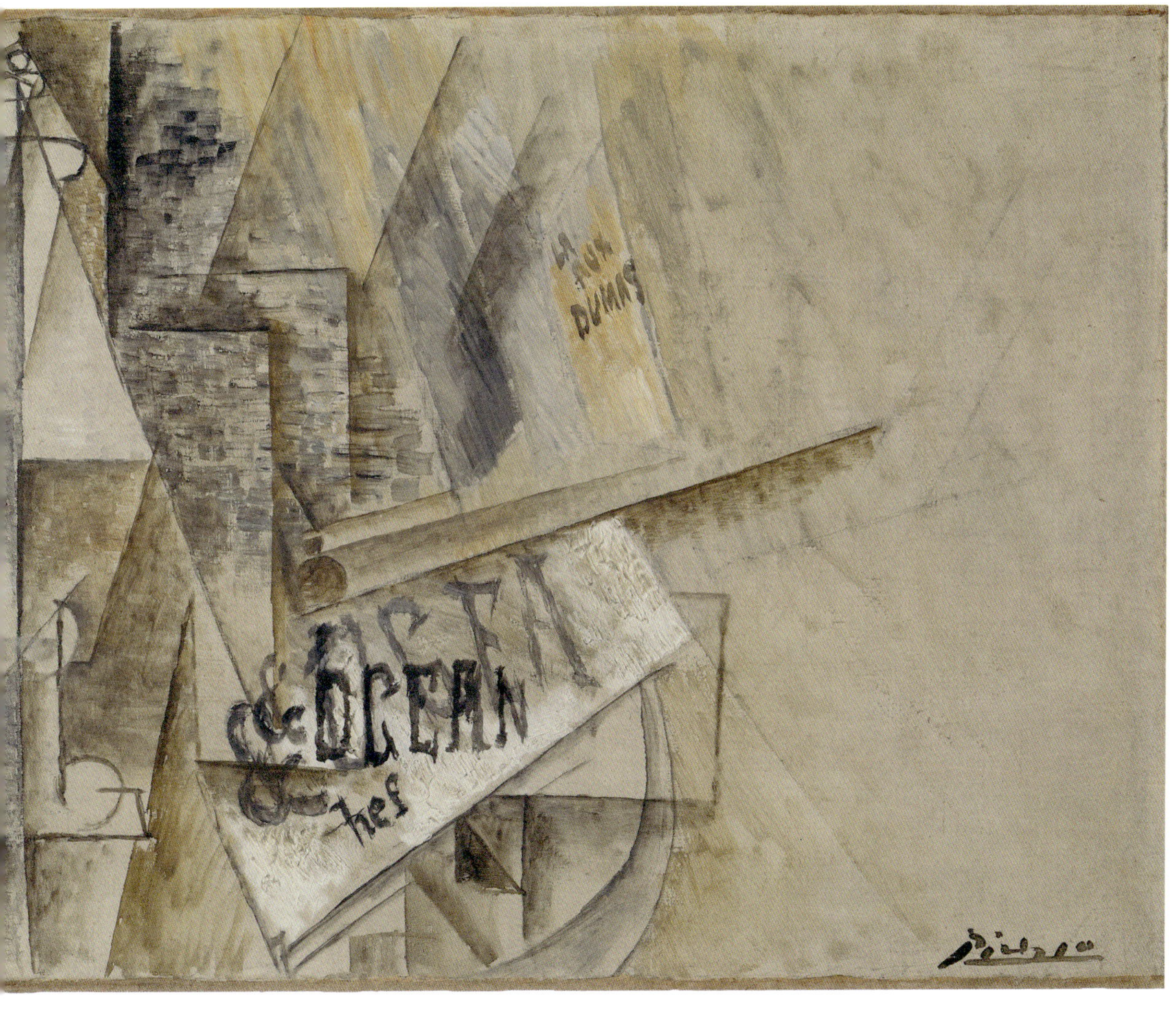
LA
DUMAS
OCEAN
hef

Plate 13
Still Life on a Piano,
summer 1911/1912

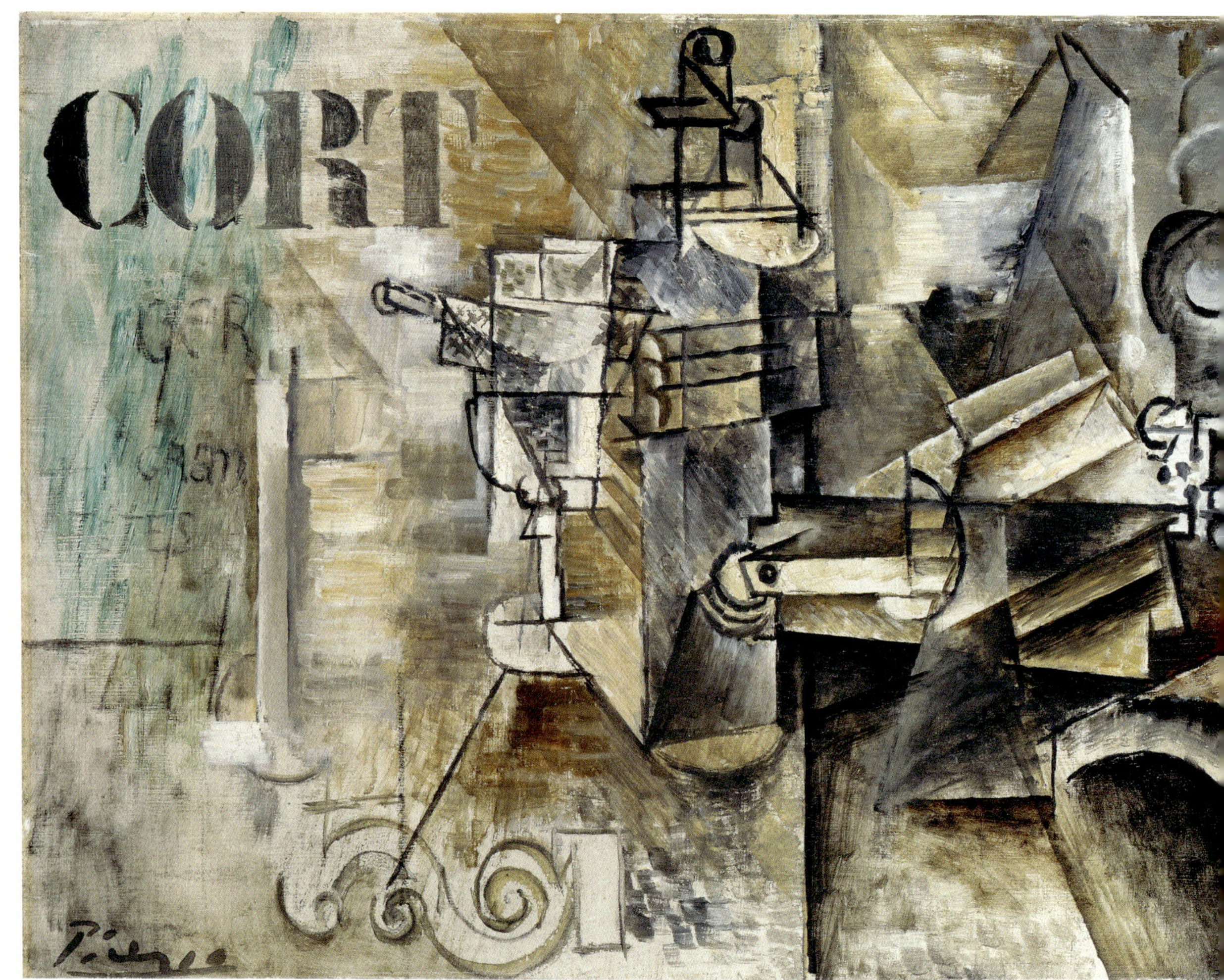

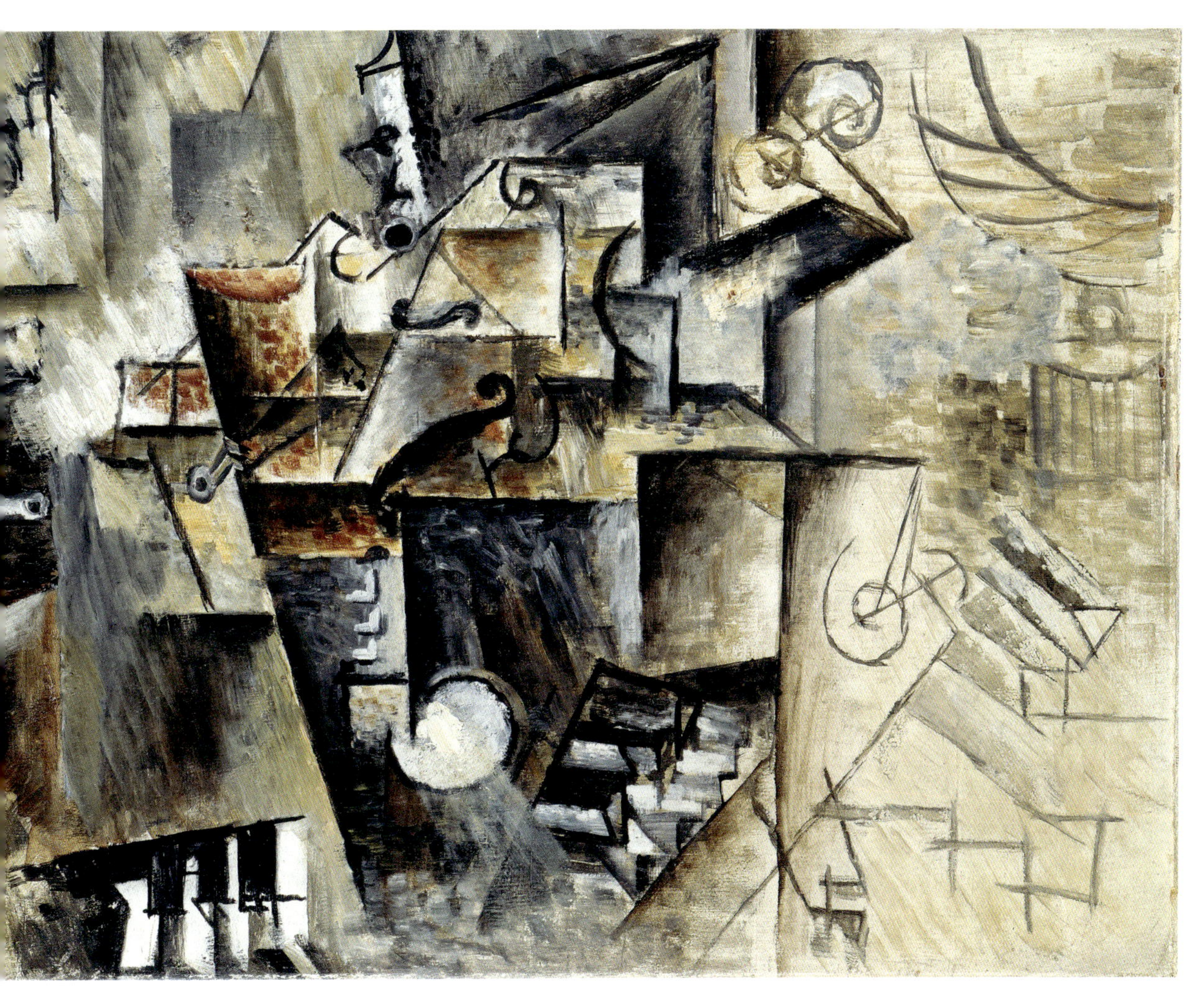

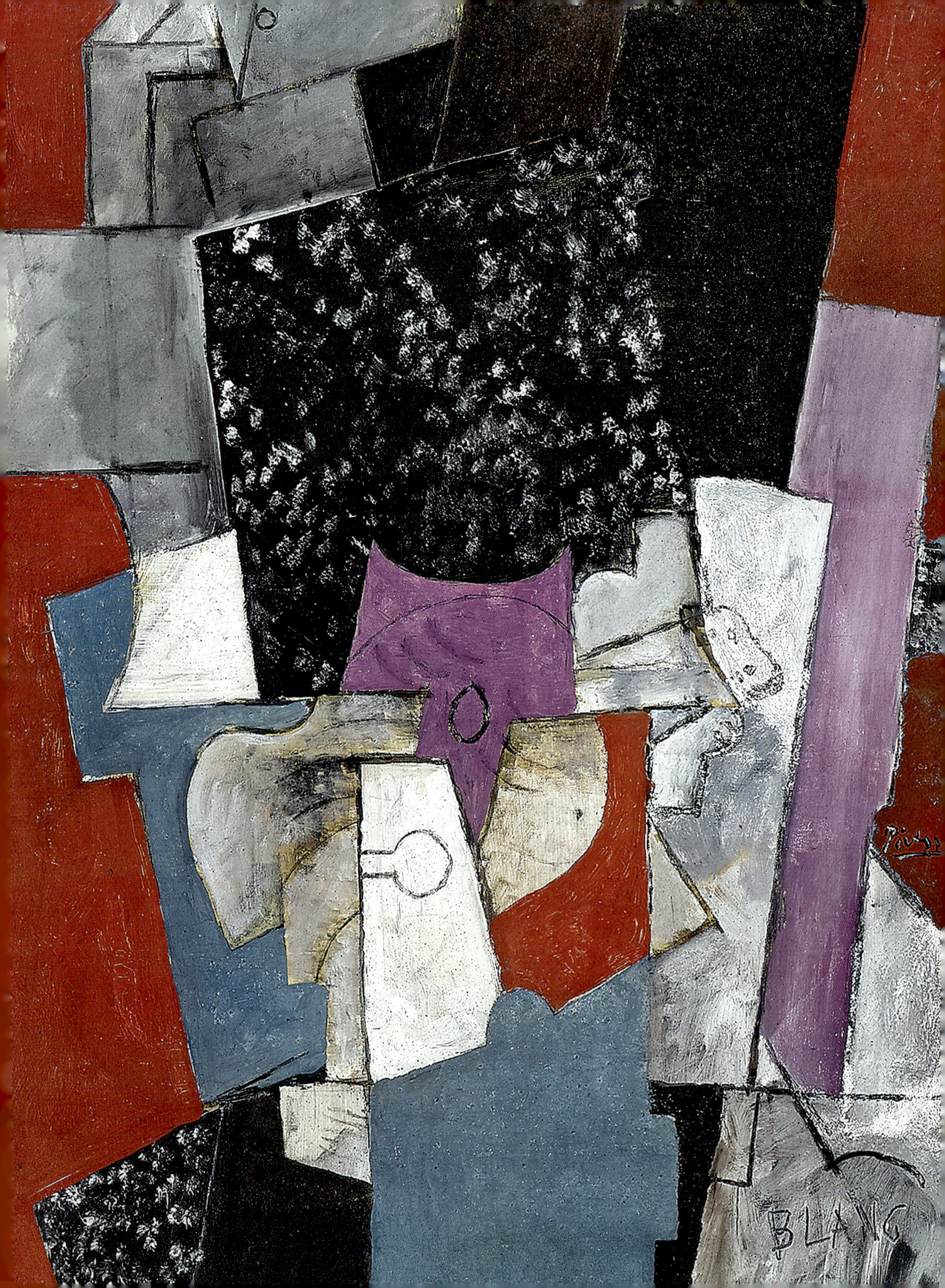
BLANC

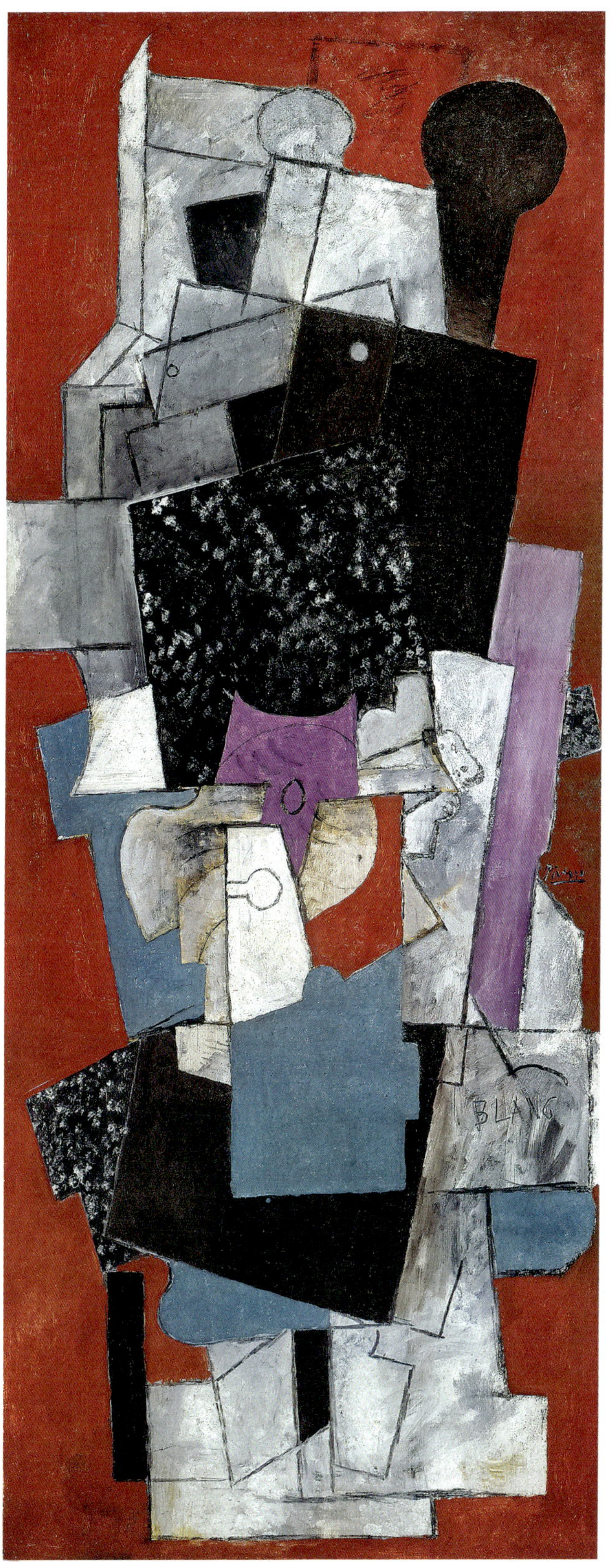

Plate 14
Woman with a Guitar, fall/winter 1915

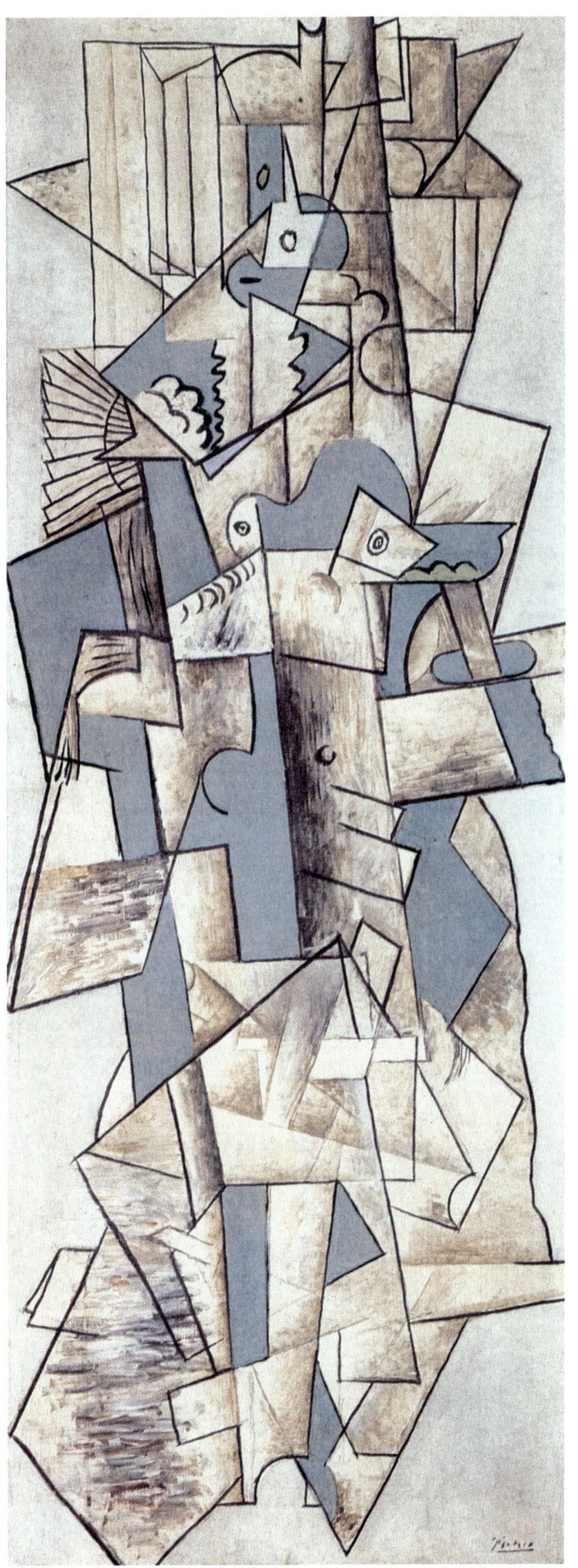

Plate 15
Woman with a Fan,
1910/1918

LIST OF WORKS

ANNA JOZEFACKA
AND LAUREN ROSATI

The entries for the Hamilton Easter Field commission paintings include select technical information as well as provenance, exhibition, and publication histories during the years immediately following their release by the artist. Full citations for publications referenced in these entries, including Pierre Daix and Joan Rosselet's 1979 catalogue raisonné of Picasso's paintings and related works, can be found in the Selected Bibliography on p. 105.

PAINTINGS ASSOCIATED WITH THE COMMISSION

Pablo Picasso (Spanish, Málaga 1881–1973 Mougins, France)
Nude Woman
Cadaqués, summer 1910, or Paris, fall 1910
Oil on canvas
$73\frac{3}{4} \times 24$ in. (187.3×61 cm)
National Gallery of Art, Washington, D.C., Ailsa Mellon Bruce Fund (1972.46.1)
Pl. 1

MARKINGS AND TECHNICAL INFORMATION
"Picasso" signed on recto at a later date in black paint at lower center left; relined

In November 1938, probably soon after acquiring it from the artist, the Parisian dealer Pierre Loeb offered this canvas to the art historian, critic, and Cubist collector Douglas Cooper, who passed on the offer, deeming the painting unfinished.[1] A few months later, it was acquired by Mary (Meric) Callery, an American sculptor then living in Paris, and a friend of Picasso since the early part of the decade. On loan from Callery, the painting appeared publicly for the first time with the title *Standing Figure* in the landmark exhibition *Picasso: Forty Years of His Art*, which opened at the Museum of Modern Art, New York, on November 15, 1939. The museum's director, Alfred H. Barr Jr.—also the exhibition's curator and the editor of the accompanying catalogue—strove to situate the painting within Picasso's stylistic development of Cubism and evaluate his turn toward abstraction. Pairing it with the charcoal drawing *Standing Female Nude* (pl. 4), on loan from Alfred Stieglitz, Barr stated: "These works are not entirely 'abstract,' they retain certain vestiges of the 'model' but these very vestiges serve to indicate the process of abstraction and lead to a more complicated aesthetic tension than is possible in purely abstract compositions of squares or circles."[2] In 1942 the painting was given its current title by Christian Zervos in his catalogue raisonné of Picasso's oeuvre.[3] The painting was subsequently owned by Carlo Frua de Angeli, Callery's friend and—briefly—husband, whose collection also included two horizontal panels: *Reclining Woman on a Sofa* and *Still Life on a Piano* (pls. 11, 13).

CATALOGUE RAISONNÉ
Daix and Rosselet 1979, no. 363, *Female Nude*, Cadaqués, summer 1910

PROVENANCE
Collection of the artist; Galerie Pierre (Pierre Loeb), Paris, by November 1938; Mary (Meric) Callery by early 1939, until at least 1945; Carlo Frua de Angeli, Milan, by 1955; his estate/heirs,1969; Galerie Beyeler (Ernst Beyeler), Basel, May 1972 (or 1970); National Gallery of Art, Washington, D.C., on Oct. 5, 1972.

Pablo Picasso
Reclining Woman on a Sofa
Paris, fall 1910
Oil on canvas
$19\frac{15}{16} \times 51$ in. (49×129.5 cm)
Private collection
Pl. 11

MARKINGS AND TECHNICAL INFORMATION
"Picasso" signed on recto at a later date with black paint at lower right; relined

The current descriptive title was first listed in Zervos's catalogue raisonné published in 1942/1944.[4] This compendium marks the painting's first appearance in print, which is also the case for the two other horizontal commission paintings, *Pipe Rack and Still Life on a Table* and *Still Life on a Piano* (pls. 12, 13). Moreover, *Reclining Woman on a Sofa* and *Still Life on a Piano* were both out of Picasso's possession by 1946, when they appeared together in an exhibition at the Kunsthaus Zürich.[5] The accompanying publication speaks to the difficulty of recognizing *Reclining Woman on a Sofa* as a figurative painting. In the published checklist the work was correctly identified with the Zervos catalogue number 727, but not the Zervos title. Instead, the painting was listed as *Composition*, which reflects the painting's highly abstract stylistic syntax.

CATALOGUE RAISONNÉ

Daix and Rosselet 1979, no. 365, *Woman Lying on a Couch*, Paris, fall 1910

PROVENANCE

Collection of the artist; Robert Meier, Zurich, by 1946; Carlo Frua de Angeli, Milan, by 1953; Alberto Ulrich, Mexico City; Galerie Beyeler (Ernst Beyeler), Basel, December 1965; Josef Steegmann, Zurich, 1968, to his daughter Mariann Steegmann, Vaduz; by descent to private collection; private collection, January 2010.

Pablo Picasso
Man with a Guitar
Céret and Paris, summer/fall 1911, reworked in 1913
Oil on canvas
60⅝ × 30½ in. (154 × 77.5 cm)
Musée National Picasso-Paris, Dation Pablo Picasso, 1979 (MP34)
Pl. 8

MARKINGS AND TECHNICAL INFORMATION

"Picasso / K 11 & 12 / ET 13" signed and dated on the reverse

Sometime in 1911 Picasso folded a large piece of canvas and used a portion of it (38⅝ by 30½ inches, or 98 by 77.5 centimeters) to execute a painting of a half-length figure holding a stringed instrument. The dealer Daniel-Henry Kahnweiler photographed and inventoried it as *Buffalo Bill*.[6] Later, in late 1911 or early 1912, Picasso took the painting back from Kahnweiler, unfolded the bottom section of the canvas, and reworked the composition until 1913 to create a large-scale painting of a full-length figure, which became known as *Man with a Guitar*. An inscription on the back notes the dates Picasso revised the canvas. After it was returned to the artist's possession in 1911, the painting never left his studio again during his lifetime. Following the artist's death in 1973, it was photographed for volume twenty-eight of the artist's catalogue raisonné, as it had been omitted from an earlier inventory of his Cubist oeuvre published during World War II by Zervos (volume two). It appears in that volume with the simplified title *Le Guitariste*.[7] The painting was first shown publicly in 1979 at the Grand Palais in Paris, in an exhibition devoted to artworks by Picasso that were accepted by the French state in lieu of inheritance taxes. It appears in that exhibition catalogue as number forty-eight under its present title, *Homme à la guitare*.[8]

CATALOGUE RAISONNÉ

Daix and Rosselet 1979, no. 427, *Man with Guitar*, Paris, fall 1911

PROVENANCE

Collection of the artist, until Apr. 8, 1973; the artist's estate (The Picasso Estate), until 1979; by donation to the Musée National Picasso-Paris.

Pablo Picasso
Man with a Mandolin
Céret and Paris, summer/fall 1911
Oil on canvas
63¾ × 27 15⁄16 in. (162 × 71 cm)
Musée National Picasso-Paris, Dation Pablo Picasso, 1979 (MP35)
Pl. 9

MARKINGS AND TECHNICAL INFORMATION

None

As with *Man with a Guitar,* Picasso worked on *Man with a Mandolin* in stages. He began a half-length figure composition in spring 1911 and then attached a piece of canvas to the bottom of the existing one to extend the form across the surface. Unlike its pendant painting, this work was publicly shown and reproduced during the artist's lifetime. In 1942 Zervos included it in the artist's catalogue raisonné published during World War II,[9] and Picasso lent the work to the 1966 exhibition *Hommage à Pablo Picasso* at the Grand Palais in Paris.[10] The following year, it traveled to a Picasso retrospective at the Stedelijk Museum in Amsterdam, where it was shown alongside two other works from the Field commission: *Reclining Woman on a Sofa* and *Still Life on a Piano* (pls. 11, 13).[11]

CATALOGUE RAISONNÉ

Daix and Rosselet 1979, no. 428, *Man with Mandoline*, Paris, fall 1911

PROVENANCE

Collection of the artist, until Apr. 8, 1973; the artist's estate (The Picasso Estate), until 1979; by donation to the Musée National Picasso-Paris.

Pablo Picasso
Pipe Rack and Still Life on a Table
Céret, summer 1911
Oil and charcoal on canvas
19½ × 50 in. (49.5 × 127 cm), irregular
20 × 50¼ in. (50.8 × 127.6 cm), mounted
The Metropolitan Museum of Art, New York, The Mr. and Mrs. Klaus G. Perls Collection, 1997 (1997.149.6)
Pl. 12

MARKINGS AND TECHNICAL INFORMATION

"Picasso" signed on recto at a later date with black paint at lower right; relined

In 1942/1944 Christian Zervos published the painting in Picasso's catalogue raisonné under the title *Pipes, Cup, Coffee-pot and Carafe*, picturing it side by side with the other two overdoor paintings from the Field commission (pls. 11, 13).[12] In 1946 *Cahiers d'Art*—the journal edited and published by Zervos—ran an announcement reproducing one painting by Henri Matisse and nine paintings by Picasso, including *Pipe Rack and Still Life on a Table*, with a note that these works "disappeared" (*disparu*) during the war.[13] While research by The Met is ongoing, at the time of this publication it is still unknown when *Pipe Rack and Still Life on a Table* left Picasso's studio and how it came to be "found." It is also unknown when and from whom it was acquired by the Galerie Georges Moos in Geneva, which sold the work to the New York dealer Klaus G. Perls in 1951. Visual inspection and comparison suggest, however, that Picasso signed the painting in the postwar period, indicating that the artist did not question the painting's re-appearance.[14] Regularly exhibited at the Perls Galleries, the painting was also lent to museum exhibitions, notably the Museum of Modern Art's *Picasso and Braque: Pioneering Cubism* (1989), the catalogue of which included the first mention of Hamilton Easter Field's commission. In 1997 Perls and his wife donated *Pipe Rack and Still Life on a Table* to The Met.

CATALOGUE RAISONNÉ

Daix and Rosselet 1979, no. 417, *Pipes, Cup, Coffee-pot and Carafe,* Céret, summer 1911(?)

PROVENANCE

Collection of the artist; Galerie Georges Moos, Geneva, by 1951; Perls Galleries (Klaus G. Perls), Oct. 8, 1951, for $8,000, stock no. 5021; donated to The Metropolitan Museum of Art by Mr. and Mrs. Klaus G. Perls, 1997.

Pablo Picasso
Still Life on a Piano
Céret, summer 1911, and Paris, 1912
Oil and charcoal on canvas
19 11⁄16 × 51 3⁄16 in. (50 × 130 cm)
Staatliche Museen zu Berlin, Nationalgalerie, Museum Berggruen
Pl. 13

MARKINGS AND TECHNICAL INFORMATION

"Picasso" signed at a later date on recto with black paint at lower left; relined

Like *Reclining Woman on a Sofa* and *Pipe Rack and Still Life on a Table* (pls. 11, 12), this overdoor painting also appeared in print for the first time in Zervos's catalogue raisonné, with the title *Absinthe glass, bottle, fan, pipe, violin, and clarinet on a piano*.[15] This painting also shares its early provenance and exhibition history with *Reclining Woman on a Sofa*. After being exhibited at the Kunsthaus Zürich in 1946, the two paintings were part of the Picasso room at the 1948 Venice Biennale.[16] Sometime after 1948 both paintings were acquired by Carlo Frua de Angeli, who had known Picasso since the early 1930s. De Angeli also came to own *Nude Woman* (pl. 1), a work that was first acquired by his friend—and briefly, wife—Mary (Meric) Callery.

CATALOGUE RAISONNÉ

Daix and Rosselet 1979, no. 462, *Piano with Still-life*, Céret, summer 1911–Paris, spring 1912(?)

PROVENANCE

Collection of the artist; Robert Meier, Zurich, by 1946; Carlo Frua de Angeli, Milan, by 1953; Christian and Yvonne Zervos, Paris; Jane Wade, New York, until 1965; Heinz Berggruen, Paris, in 1965; Museum Berggruen, Berlin.

Pablo Picasso

Woman with a Guitar

Paris, fall/winter 1915

Oil on canvas

72 ⅞ × 29 ⅝ in. (185 × 75 cm)

Callimanopulos Collection

*not included in the exhibition

Pl. 14

MARKINGS AND TECHNICAL INFORMATION

"Picasso" signed on recto with black paint at center right

This painting, with its figure rendered in large planes of bright colors and varied textures set against a red monochromatic background, formally departs from the style of the other commission panels. Picasso composed the central figure in almost sculptural terms with parts that seem to twist and bend, a quality that may link it to his painted sheet-metal sculptures of the same year. Walter P. Chrysler Jr. acquired the painting by 1938, the year when he lent it to an exhibition of Picasso's work at the now-defunct Boston Museum of Modern Art, where it was shown—alongside works by Henri Matisse—as *Abstraction*, with an incorrect date of 1921.[17] By the time of its inclusion in Picasso's catalogue raisonné published by Christian Zervos in 1942/1944, the work had received its present date and title, *Femme à la guitare*.[18]

CATALOGUE RAISONNÉ

Daix and Rosselet 1979, no. 843, *Woman with Guitar*, Paris, fall or late 1915

PROVENANCE

Collection of the artist; Galerie Pierre (Pierre Loeb), Paris; Walter P. Chrysler Jr., New York; Ragnar Moltzau, Oslo, by Feb. 1957; Marlborough Fine Art Ltd., London; Norton Simon, Los Angeles (Christie, Manson & Woods International Inc., sale, Oct. 21, 1980, lot 203); Callimanopulos Collection (Gregory Callimanopulos).

Pablo Picasso

Woman with a Fan

Paris, 1910/1918

Oil on canvas

72 ⅞ × 28 ⅝ in. (185 × 72.5 cm)

Private collection

*not included in the exhibition

Pl. 15

MARKINGS AND TECHNICAL INFORMATION

"Picasso" signed on recto with black paint at lower right

A reproduction of *Woman with a Fan* in a 1937 advertisement for Galerie Pierre suggests that Picasso sold the painting to Pierre Loeb around the same time as two other paintings associated with the commission: *Nude Woman* and *Woman with a Guitar* (pls. 1, 14).[19] In 1944 the New York art dealer Valentine Dudensing used it in a Valentine Gallery advertisement in *View* magazine,[20] updating Loeb's title *Peinture* to the current title, which was also the same one published in Zervos's catalogue raisonné.[21] New York collector Emily Hall Spreckels, soon to be married to Burton Tremaine, with whom she formed an important collection of modern and contemporary art, purchased the work from Dudensing in November. *Woman with a Fan* appeared in the 1948 traveling exhibition *Painting toward Architecture*—developed by the Tremaines using their collection—which explored links between modern art and architecture through the lens of abstraction. The accompanying publication addressed Picasso's two painting campaigns that resulted in two overlapping, but distinct, compositions: "The underlying painting on this canvas, dating from 1911 [*sic*], breaks up the forms of the human figure into a series of planes set at angles and rendered in delicate touches of near monochrome. This phase of cubism was more sculptural than architectonic in character. Over this painting Picasso in 1918 laid a vigorous pattern of black lines and flat blue areas in the larger-scaled and clarified manner of the later stage of the cubist development. It was from this later synthetic stage of cubism, beginning about 1913, that the abstract artists took off [and] who were most closely associated with the crystallization of the forms of a new architecture in the early 1920s."[22]

CATALOGUE RAISONNÉ

Daix and Rosselet 1979, no. 364, *Woman with Fan*, Cadaqués, summer 1910 (finished 1918)

PROVENANCE

Collection of the artist; Galerie Pierre (Pierre Loeb), Paris, by 1937; Valentine Gallery (Valentine Dudensing), New York, inv. no. 2640, for $4,000, between May and Nov. 1944; Emily Hall Spreckels (Emily Hall Tremaine as of 1945), Santa Barbara, Nov. 1944, purchased for $8,000 or $8,500; the Tremaine Collection (Emily Hall Tremaine and Burton Tremaine), 1945–87; sold by Emily Hall Tremaine through Gagosian Gallery (Larry Gagosian), New York, March 12, 1987; private collection.

RELATED PAINTINGS AND WORKS ON PAPER

Pablo Picasso
Female Nude
Paris, spring 1910
Watercolor, pen, and ink on paper
29 1/8 × 18 1/4 in. (74 × 46.4 cm)
Private collection
Pl. 2

Pablo Picasso
Standing Nude
Cadaqués, summer 1910
Ink on paper
12 1/2 × 8 1/2 in. (31.8 × 21.6 cm)
Private collection, New York
Pl. 3

Pablo Picasso
Standing Female Nude
Cadaqués, summer 1910
Ink on white wove paper
12 1/4 × 8 1/8 in. (31.1 × 20.6 cm)
The Metropolitan Museum of Art, New York, Leonard A. Lauder Cubist Collection, Gift of Leonard A. Lauder, 2016 (2016.237.31)
Pl. 4

Pablo Picasso
Nude
Cadaqués, summer 1910
Ink on paper
12 3/8 × 8 1/4 in. (31.5 × 20.9 cm)
Staatsgalerie Stuttgart, Graphische Sammlung, 1965 (1966/1438)
Pl. 5

Pablo Picasso
Standing Nude Woman
Cadaqués, summer 1910, or Paris, fall 1910
Oil on canvas
10 7/16 × 5 7/8 in. (26.5 × 15 cm)
Fundación Almine y Bernard Ruiz-Picasso para el Arte, Madrid
Pl. 6

Pablo Picasso
Standing Female Nude
Paris, fall 1910
Charcoal on paper
19 × 12 3/8 in. (48.3 × 31.4 cm)
The Metropolitan Museum of Art, New York, Alfred Stieglitz Collection, 1949 (49.70.34)
Pl. 7

Pablo Picasso
Standing Woman
Sorgues, summer 1912
Ink, charcoal dipped in oil, and gouache on two sheets of off-white wove paper
21 11/16 × 8 9/16 in. (55 × 21.7 cm)
The Metropolitan Museum of Art, New York, Leonard A. Lauder Cubist Collection, Gift of Leonard A. Lauder, 2016 (2016.237.34)
Pl. 10

WORKS OWNED BY HAMILTON EASTER FIELD

Pablo Picasso
Study of a Nude Woman
ca. 1905–6
Pen and gray-brown ink on paper
14 15⁄16 × 10 1⁄16 in. (38 × 25.6 cm)
Museum of Fine Arts, Boston, John H. and Ernestine A. Payne Fund (1970.578)
Fig. 34

Robert Laurent (American, born Concarneau, France, 1890–1970 Cape Neddick, Maine)
Balloons
Brooklyn, 1913
Walnut
9 × 65 3⁄4 × 7⁄8 in. (22.8 × 167 × 2.2 cm)
Private collection
Fig. 16

DOCUMENTARY MATERIAL

Hamilton Easter Field (American, Brooklyn 1873–1922 Brooklyn)
Letter from Hamilton Easter Field to Pablo Picasso
postmarked Brooklyn, July 12, 1910
Ink on paper, two double-sided sheets with envelope
Each sheet: 6 11⁄16 × 9 5⁄8 in. (16.7 × 24.5 cm)
Envelope: 3 7⁄16 × 5 1⁄8 in. (8.8 × 13 cm)
Musée National Picasso-Paris, Don succession Pablo Picasso, 1992 (SISAP/C/47/28/1 [1, 2])
P. 90

"Brooklyn Bridge, from Brooklyn, N.Y."
ca. 1910
Lithographic postcard
3 1⁄2 × 5 1⁄2 in. (8.9 × 14 cm)
The Bob Stonehill Postcard Collection
Fig. 8

"Columbia Heights, Brooklyn"
ca. 1910
Lithographic postcard
3 1⁄2 × 5 1⁄2 in. (8.9 × 14 cm)
The Bob Stonehill Postcard Collection
*not illustrated

Eugene L. Armbruster (American, born Baden-Baden, Germany, 1865–1943 Brooklyn)
Brooklyn: Roebling House, 110 Columbia Heights, between Orange Street and Pineapple Street
1922
Photographic print
7 × 5 in. (17.8 × 12.7 cm)
New-York Historical Society, Eugene L. Armbruster Photograph Collection, 1894–1939
Fig. 9

CHRONOLOGY OF THE COMMISSION, 1909–22

ANNA JOZEFACKA AND LAUREN ROSATI

February 13–26, 1909
Hamilton Easter Field and his mother, Lydia Seaman Haviland Field, sail together to Europe, arriving by February 26.[1] They remain there for more than a year and a half, staying primarily in Italy, but also traveling to England, France, and Switzerland. Thus far, their precise itinerary can be only partially reconstructed.

In 1919 Field recounted visiting Pablo Picasso in Paris in 1909.[2] While the fall is the most likely time of this meeting, spring—after Field arrives in Europe and before Picasso leaves Paris for the summer—cannot be ruled out.

Early May 1909
In Paris since early September 1908, Picasso and his companion Fernande Olivier leave for Spain, where they remain for four months.

July 1, 1909
Field and his mother are reported to be spending the summer in Florence.[3]

Around September 11, 1909
Picasso and Olivier return to Paris and move from their meager quarters at Bateau-Lavoir, rue Ravignan, to a top-floor apartment with an airy studio at 11 boulevard de Clichy. Picasso remains in Paris for more than nine months.

October 16, 1909
A *Brooklyn Life* column chronicling Brooklynites in Paris reports on Field and his mother's winter plans, allowing speculation that they have been in the French capital for some time.[4] This seems a likely moment for Field's meeting with Picasso about the commission at the artist's boulevard de Clichy apartment.[5] He is probably introduced to Picasso by Frank Burty Haviland—his cousin, a painter, and the Spaniard's friend and patron—who was in Paris by the end of September or beginning of October.[6] Probably present is Field's protégé, the French-born American sculptor Robert Laurent, at that time training to become an artist. Field recalled the meeting in 1919: "In my enthusiasm over his [Picasso's] work I went to him in 1909 and told him that it seemed to me that he made a mistake in merely painting easel pictures, for abstract art needed an entire room or better a house in which all furniture should be subordinated to the decorations which would cover the flat walls. He should get orders to decorate buildings. I could not offer him a house to decorate, but I had a library with no pieces of furniture except the bookshelves and a few low chairs."[7] According to Laurent, who in 1966 recalled also being present at the meeting, Picasso was "excited" to receive "just the sort of commission he had been hoping for."[8]

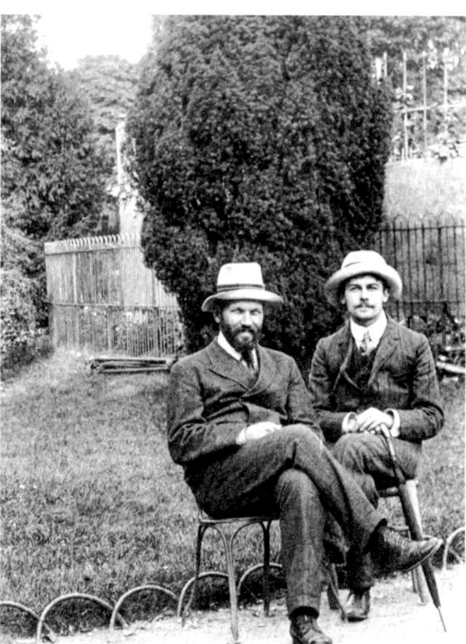

Hamilton Easter Field and Robert Laurent, Europe, ca. 1910. Barn Gallery Associates selected records, 1966–1987, Archives of American Art, Smithsonian Institution, Washington, D.C.

November 1909–May 1910
Field and his mother spend the winter and spring in Rome.[9] Field keeps a studio at via Margutta and socializes with the American painter and sculptor Maurice Sterne.[10]

Between May 16 and 22, 1910
Field and his mother stop in Paris on their way from Rome to Southampton, England, where they will board a steamship bound for New York the following month.[11] There, Field probably meets again with Picasso, giving them a chance to further discuss the commissioned suite of decorative panels for Field's library as well as mutual acquaintances, among them Sterne.

June 15–23, 1910
Field and his mother sail back to New York from Southampton, England.[12]

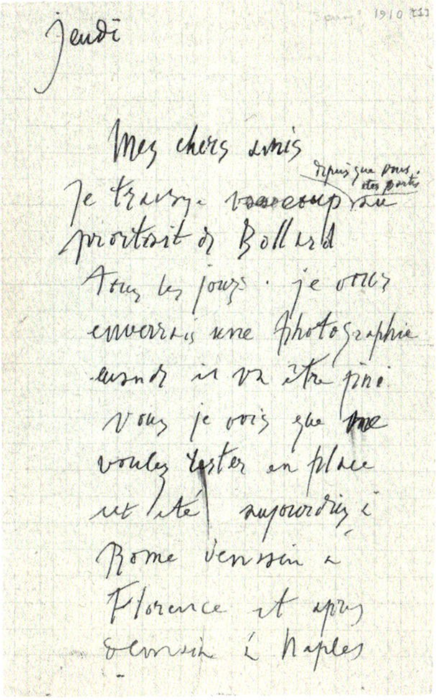

Letter from Pablo Picasso to Gertrude Stein, undated [June 1910?]. One sheet, double-sided, handwritten, approx. 6 × 4 in. (15.2 × 10.2 cm). Gertrude Stein and Alice B. Toklas Papers, Yale Collection of American Literature, Beinecke Rare Book and Manuscript Library, Yale University, New Haven

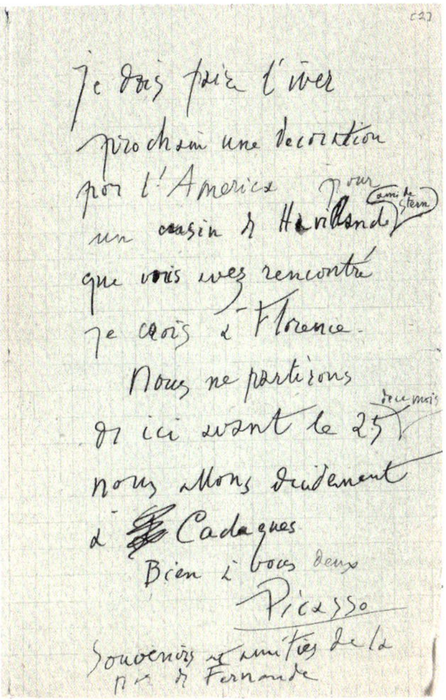

Around June 16, 1910

Preparing to leave Paris for the summer in Cadaqués, Spain, Picasso writes an undated letter to his friend and patron Gertrude Stein in Florence about his approaching travel plans. In it, he also mentions the commission: "Next winter I have to do a decoration for America, for a cousin of [Frank Burty] Haviland's (friend of [Maurice] Sterne's) whom you've met in Florence I believe."[13]

July 12, 1910

After arriving in Brooklyn, Field mails to Picasso a letter written in French with details about the commission and includes sketches of a wall elevation, the floor plan of the room, and diagrams of the panel sizes. The letter, addressed to Picasso, care of Frank Burty Haviland in Paris, reads:

> Dear Sir,
>
> I send you all the necessary indications for the decoration project. The library is a room 7 meters by 3 with a single window at one end. The window is rather large and the room is quite bright — except for panel H which is a bit dark. At night all the panels will be well lit with electricity. I don't think the decoration of panel H should be somehow changed because of its position. The color contrasts should not be too delicate. But otherwise there is no reason to modify it. When I saw you I thought wall F was so narrow that there was no need for decoration there and that I would fill it with a wooden panel — If you think it would be better to make a decorative panel I leave it entirely up to you. As you know, in any case I give you complete freedom. Do whatever you think best suited to the room. The decorations will be seen close-up (the room is rather narrow) and the shelves with books circle the entire library.
>
> Apologies for my mistakes — I am not used to writing in French. My friends are keenly interested in your decorations — especially the painter [Arthur B.] Davies who wants to see your pictures — He is a charming man who will be spending ten or so days in Paris in October. He is going there expressly to see what the youngsters are up to —
>
> With best wishes to you and your wife —
> Hamilton Field[14]

Letter from Hamilton Easter Field to Pablo Picasso, postmarked July 12, 1910. Ink on paper, two double-sided sheets with envelope; each sheet: 6 11/16 × 9 5/8 in. (16.7 × 24.5 cm); envelope: 3 7/16 × 5 1/8 in. (8.8 × 13 cm). Musée National Picasso-Paris, Don succession Pablo Picasso, 1992 (SISAP/C/47/28/1 [1, 2])

106 Columbia Heights.
Brooklyn.
New York

Cher monsieur -

Je vous envoie toutes les indications necessaires pour le projet de decoration - La bibliothèque est une chambre 7 mètres sur 3 éclairée d'une seule fenetre au bout. La fenetre est assez grand et la piece est bien éclairée - sauf le panneau H qui est un peu sombre. Le soir tous les panneaux seront bien illuminés avec l'electricité - Je ne crois pas que la decoration du panneau H doit avoir quelque modification à cause de sa position - Les contrasts de couleurs ne doivent pas être trop delicats

mais autrement il n'y a pas de raison pour une modification.

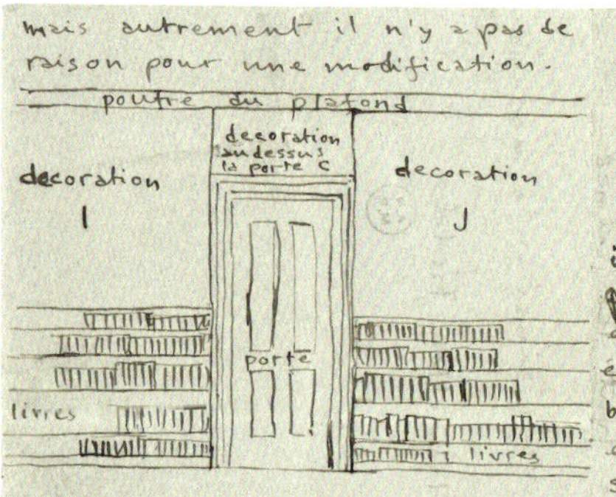

Quand je vous ai vu je croyais que le mur F était si étroit qu'il n'y avait pas besoin de decoration et que je le remplirais avec ~~du~~ un panneau de bois - Si vous croyez que ça serait mieux de faire un panneau decoratif je vous ~~serai~~ donne entière liberté

Comme vous savez du reste je veux vous laisser libre - Faites ce que vous trouverez sera le plus adapté à la piece - Les decorations seront vus de près (la chambre étant assez étroite) et les planches avec les livres vont tout au tour de la bibliothèque -

Pardonnez moi mes fautes - Je n'ai pas l'habitude d'ecrire en français. Mes amis s'interessent vivement à vos decorations - surtout le peintre Davies qui veut voir vos tableaux - C'est un homme charmant qui va passer une dizaine de jours à Paris en octobre. Il y va exprès pour voir ce que font les jeunes -

Bien à vous ainsi qu'à madame -

Hamilton Field

A.N. M.P.

1/3 SISAP/C/47/28/1(1)

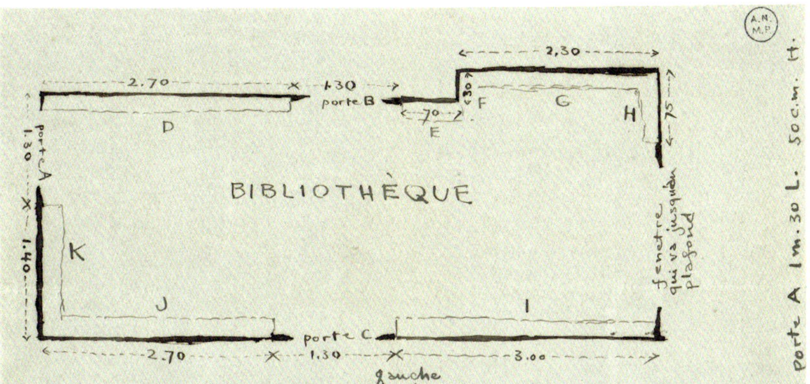

En entrant par la porte A il y a à ~~droite~~ gauche un panneau en largeur 2m.70 L. 1m.85 H. Au dessus de la porte B un panneau 1M.30 L. 50c.m. H. Ensuite le panneau E 70 c.m. Largeur 1M.85 H le panneau F 30 c.m. L. 1.85 H. le panneau G 2m.30 L. 1M.85 H. le panneau H — 75 c.m. L. 1m.85 H. On passe la fenetre – En face le plus grand panneau I 3 metres large. 1.85 H. Au dessus de la porte C un panneau 130 c.m. L. 50 c.m. H. le panneau J 2m.70 L. 1m.85 Hauteur le panneau K 1.40 L. 1m.85 H. le panneau au dessus

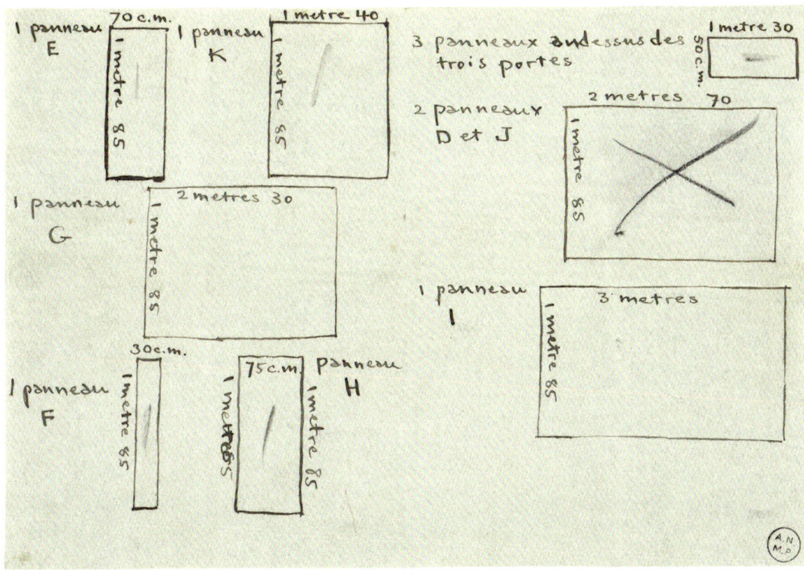

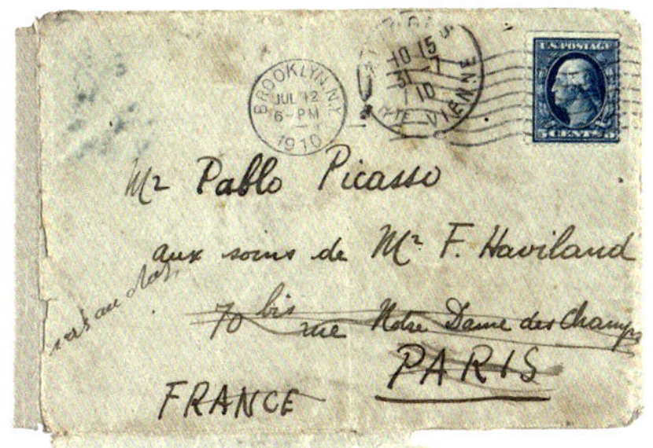

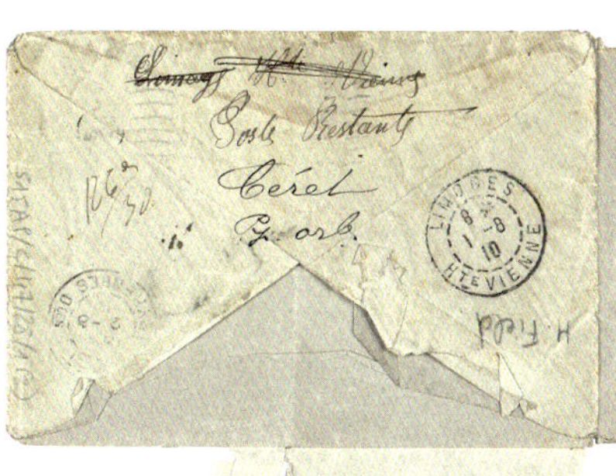

In the legend for the floor plan, Field lists eleven wall areas and identifies them with the letters A through K. Each requires an unusually sized and proportioned canvas: three oblong horizontals (50 × 130 centimeters each), to be installed over the three doorways, two large horizontals (185 × 270 centimeters each), one mural-size canvas (185 × 300 centimeters), and five additional panels with vertical orientations, all 185 centimeters tall but with varying widths (30, 70, 75, 140, and 230 centimeters).

The designated room is located on the main (parlor) level of the Field residence toward the rear of the building, accessible from both the hallway and the back parlor. According to Field's drawing, low shelves line the room, presumably holding a portion of his vast collection of rare art and literary volumes, first-edition books, and sheet music.

August 2, 1910
Picasso receives the letter from Field sometime after this date, while still in Cadaqués. The envelope bears several inscriptions and postal stamps documenting its journey from Brooklyn to Céret, where Burty Haviland was then staying.

August 13–25, 1910
Before leaving Cadaqués, Picasso photographs some of his summer paintings (fig. 17). The photograph shows a currently unaccounted-for large composition of a standing figure executed on an unstretched canvas pinned to a wall—perhaps Picasso's initial attempt at the commission. He possibly paints *Nude Woman* (pl. 1) and *Woman with a Fan* (pl. 15).

September 1, 1910
Again in Paris, Picasso replies to Field in French. The note reads:

> 11 Boulevard de Clichy
>
> Dear Sir,
> I received your letter in Spain. I am back in Paris and think I will soon begin work for your library. The plan that you sent me is very clear. I will be very happy to meet your friend the painter Davies.
>
> Kind regards
> Picasso
> Paris Thursday 1 September 1910[15]

Fall 1910–winter 1911
By this period, Picasso completes the first panels for the commission: the narrow vertical

11 Boulevard de Clichy

Cher Monsieur
J'ai reçu votre lettre en Espagne. Je suis de retour à Paris et bientot je pense commencer les travaux pour votre bibliotheque.
Le plan que vous m'avez envoyé est tres clair.
Je serai tres heureux de connaitre votre ami le

le peintre Davies.
Bien à vous
Picasso

Paris Jeudi 1 Septembre 1910

Letter from Pablo Picasso to Hamilton Easter Field, September 1, 1910. Private collection

Nude Woman (pl. 1)—a candidate for wall E—and *Woman with a Fan* (pl. 15)—perhaps for wall H—to which he will return eight years later. He also completes the first of three horizontal overdoors, *Reclining Woman on a Sofa* (pl. 11)—intended possibly for door A. All of these depict highly abstract female figures.

At some point, Picasso probably annotates the page of Field's letter containing a diagram of panel sizes with vertical "I" and "X" pencil markings over certain panels. He holds on to this letter his entire life.

Spring 1911
The artist starts on two figure paintings, *Man with a Guitar* and *Man with a Mandolin* (pls. 8, 9), both of which he subsequently enlarges, almost doubling their sizes to produce vertical canvases of full-length figures.

March 28–April 25, 1911
In New York photographer and staunch promoter of modern art Alfred Stieglitz presents Picasso's work for the first time in the United States in a show of eighty-three drawings and watercolors at his Photo-Secession Galleries, better known as 291. Field visits the exhibition—multiple times, according to Stieglitz's later recollection[16]—and purchases a pen-and-ink *Study of a Nude Woman* from about 1905–6 (fig. 34). Besides Stieglitz himself, Field is the only other buyer from the exhibition.

July 16, 1911
In early July Picasso leaves Paris for Céret, where Frank Burty Haviland is already settled for the summer. On this date Picasso writes to the dealer Daniel-Henry Kahnweiler that he is using a large room at Burty Haviland's house rental as his temporary studio.

July 25, 1911
Picasso mentions a "big painting" in a letter to Georges Braque, who is in Paris. He notes that the picture remains "to be done" and describes it as "a stream in the middle of a town with some girls [?] swimming . . . and houses with round windows and dark transparent holes [?] full of light round houses and very square houses (but what language)."[17] William Rubin, as well as Picasso's biographer John Richardson, described this work as one destined for Field's library. Rubin did not speculate as to the possible location of this painting within the library, but, given Field's diagram, it must have been intended for wall D, G, I, or J—all areas with widths in excess of two meters.

Picasso also turns his attention to the two remaining overdoor paintings, which he eventually executes as a pair of still lifes, *Pipe Rack and Still Life on a Table* and *Still Life on a Piano* (pls. 12, 13). Created for doors B and C, they would have been positioned across from each other. He returns to the latter the following spring.

Fall 1911
A photograph taken in Picasso's boulevard de Clichy studio in Paris shows the artist standing beside several Cubist canvases, including a mural-size work fastened to a wall that could correspond to the "big painting" Picasso describes in his July 25 letter to Braque (fig. 22).

Two other photographs taken by Picasso in his studio in the boulevard de Clichy that fall show the painter Marie Laurencin posing with a mandolin next to the already enlarged but still unfinished *Man with a Mandolin* (figs. 19, 20).

September 1911
During his trip to France from August to the end of September, Stieglitz visits Picasso in Paris, where he sees some of the Field commission panels in progress. He likely informs Picasso that Field acquired a work from the artist's exhibition in New York.

October 21, 1911
Back in New York, Stieglitz writes to Field to finalize the transaction of the drawing purchased from Picasso's exhibition at 291:

> New York Oct. 21, 1911.
> My dear Field:
>
> I hope you safely received the Picasso drawing which I had 'Of' [frame store Geo. [rge] F. Of] send over to you on Monday last. The amount I laid out for you was $35.00. In Paris I saw your panels started. They promise much.

I hope to see you sometime when you have a few spare moments for '291'.

With kindest regards, I am,
Yours very truly,
[unsigned][18]

October 25, 1911
Field responds to Stieglitz with payment for the drawing; the commission goes unmentioned.

Winter 1911–12
Picasso resumes painting *Man with a Mandolin* and continues work on *Man with a Guitar*. He will finalize the latter in spring/summer 1913.

Spring 1912
Picasso completes *Still Life on a Piano*. By May 20, he is back in Céret, where he remains for a month with his new companion, Marcelle Humbert, known as Eva Gouel.

June 5, 1912
In a letter to Kahnweiler, Picasso includes the inventory of twenty-three paintings stored at his auxiliary studio at Bateau-Lavoir, rue Ravignan. He describes painting number twenty-three as "le grand paneau [*sic*] pour l'Amérique" (the large panel for America).[19]

New York Oct. 21, 1911.

My dear Mr. Field:

I hope you safely received the Picasso drawing which I had "Of" send over to you on Monday last. The amount I laid out for you was $35.00. In Paris I saw your panels started. They promise much.

I hope to see you sometime when you have a few spare moments for "291".

With kindest regards, I am,

Yours very truly,

Mr. Hamilton Field,
106 Columbia Hts.,
Brooklyn, N. Y.

Letter from Alfred Stieglitz to Hamilton Easter Field, October 21, 1911. One sheet, single-sided, typed and unsigned, approx. 11 × 8½ in. (27.9 × 21.6 cm). Alfred Stieglitz/ Georgia O'Keeffe Archive, Yale Collection of American Literature, Beinecke Rare Book and Manuscript Library, Yale University, New Haven

106 COLUMBIA HEIGHTS
BROOKLYN, NEW YORK

October 25 – 1911

My dear Mr. Stieglitz –

Enclosed my check in payment for the Picasso drawing which is a beauty – there is no need of acknowledging its receipt. I hope to be up to see you before long –

Sincerely Yours –
Hamilton Easter Field

Letter from Hamilton Easter Field to Alfred Stieglitz, October 25, 1911. One sheet, single-sided, handwritten and signed, approx. 8½ × 11 in. (21.6 × 27.9 cm). Alfred Stieglitz/ Georgia O'Keeffe Archive, Yale Collection of American Literature, Beinecke Rare Book and Manuscript Library, Yale University, New Haven

December 18, 1912–fall 1913
In December, nearly three months after moving to a new apartment and studio at 242 boulevard Raspail in Montparnasse, Picasso signs a contract with Kahnweiler, giving him exclusive rights to Picasso's artistic production for three years, but notes that he will retain "the right to accept commissions for portraits and large decorations destined for a specific place."[20]

Before the artist changes his Paris address yet again to 5 bis rue Schoelcher at the beginning of October 1913, a photograph is taken showing Picasso with a large oblong figure painting (fig. 21). The size and proportions of this thus far unaccounted-for canvas appear to correspond to either panel E or H noted in Field's letter.

Fall–winter 1915
Five years after receiving Field's commission, Picasso paints *Woman with a Guitar* (pl. 14), a work with measurements conforming to panel H (185 × 75 centimeters).

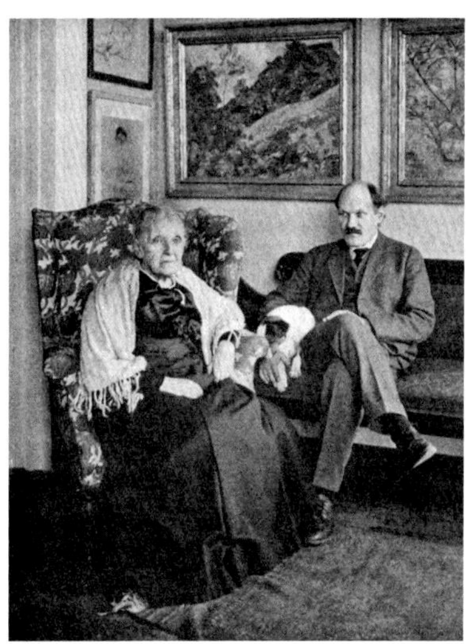

Mrs. Aaron Field and Her Son, Hamilton Easter Field, *Brooklyn Life*, March 25, 1916. Brooklyn Public Library, Center for Brooklyn History

November 12, 1917
Field's mother dies at the family residence at 106 Columbia Heights.[21] The art critic Henry McBride, an acquaintance of Field and visitor to his house, later recalled being told confidentially of the commission and being given the explanation that "the decorations [by Picasso] could not be installed during the life-time of his [Field's] mother, for it would be too much to ask for her to accustom herself to such extraordinary work."[22]

1918
Picasso revisits *Woman with a Fan* of 1910, one of the first panels he executed for the commission, and augments the work with a new compositional layer of heavy black contour lines and planes of blue and white colors.

November 30, 1919
Between March 1919 and his death in April 1922, Field writes seasonal weekly art columns for the *Brooklyn Daily Eagle*. In them, he intermittently makes references to his interactions with Picasso a decade prior. On this date, embedded within a review of a Man Ray exhibition, Field recounts offering Picasso the commission and notes that the artist's "decorations are not yet finished" for his library.[23]

June–July 1920
Field makes a trip to Europe, and published reports of his travels note that he visits Belgium, England, France, Germany, and Italy. He does not mention Picasso in the context of this trip.

April 9, 1922
Field, age forty-nine, dies at home of pneumonia, naming Robert Laurent his heir.[24] Some of his collections, including the partial contents of his library, are sold at auction by the end of the year.[25] The house at 106 Columbia Heights remains in Laurent's possession until it is acquired by the city and demolished in 1947 to make way for the Brooklyn-Queens Expressway (BQE) and a system of public park areas.[26] Today, the site of the house and adjacent properties is the Fruit Street Sitting Area.

Picasso: A Cubist Commission in Brooklyn

1. Hamilton Easter Field to Pablo Picasso, July 12, 1910, Picasso Archive, Musée National Picasso-Paris, C 1-177, classeur 47. The 1910 letter was first documented (with an erroneous date) in Judith Cousins and Hélène Seckel, "Eléments pour une chronologie de l'histoire des Demoiselles d'Avignon," in *Les Demoiselles d'Avignon*, ed. Hélène Seckel, vol. 2, exh. cat., Musée Picasso, Paris (Paris: Editions de la Réunion des Musées Nationaux, 1988), pp. 565–66.

2. The context of this discovery was William Rubin's and Judith Cousins's research for the exhibition *Picasso and Braque: Pioneering Cubism*, organized by the Museum of Modern Art, New York, in 1989. See William Rubin, "Appendix: The Library of Hamilton Easter Field," and Judith Cousins with the collaboration of Pierre Daix, "Documentary Chronology," in William Rubin, *Picasso and Braque: Pioneering Cubism*, exh. cat. (New York: Museum of Modern Art, 1989), pp. 63–69 and pp. 335–445, respectively. Rubin did not personally consult the 1910 letter for his 1989 publication. However insightful and groundbreaking, his text contains factual errors regarding the number of panels and physical details about the room. It is important to acknowledge that, prior to Rubin, at least one other art historian pursued research on the Field commission, in the late 1960s: John H. Field, a distant relative of Hamilton Easter Field. Unlike Rubin, he had no knowledge of Field's letter to Picasso, and the starting point of his investigation was Robert Laurent's recollection of the commission. See Robert Laurent, "A Personal Statement," in *The Hamilton Easter Field Art Foundation Collection*, exh. cat. (Ogunquit, Maine: Barn Gallery Associates, 1966), n.p. The author would like to thank John H. Field for his generosity in sharing his personal archives and discussing his research with her.

3. Rubin, "Appendix," p. 64.

4. Ibid.

5. John Richardson with the collaboration of Marilyn McCully, *A Life of Picasso*, vol. 2, *The Cubist Rebel, 1907–1916* (New York: Random House, 1996), pp. 164–72, 456–57; reprinted as *A Life of Picasso: The Cubist Rebel, 1907–1916* (New York: Alfred A. Knopf, 2007). Richardson also included new information about Hamilton Easter Field, which he obtained from John H. Field.

6. For Hamilton Easter Field's life and career, see, for example, Wendy Jeffers, "Hamilton Easter Field: The Benefactor from Brooklyn," *Archives of American Art Journal* 50, no. 1/2 (Spring 2011), pp. 26–37; Doreen Bolger, "Hamilton Easter Field and His Contribution to American Modernism," *American Art Journal* (Kennedy Galleries) 20, no. 2 (1988), pp. 78–107; Doreen Bolger, "Hamilton Easter Field and the Rise of Modern Art in America" (master's thesis, University of Delaware, 1973). For additional perspectives on Field, see also Hugh Ryan, *When Brooklyn Was Queer* (New York: St. Martin's Press, 2019), pp. 133–36; and Colin B. Burke, *Information and Intrigue: From Index Cards to Dewey Decimals to Alger Hiss* (Cambridge, Mass.: MIT Press, 2014).

7. The Travelers, *Brooklyn Life*, February 20, 1909, p. 20; The Travelers, *Brooklyn Life*, May 14, 1910, p. 18.

8. The Travelers, *Brooklyn Life*, October 16, 1909, p. 16. The report provided the future travel plans of Brooklyn residents who "have been in Paris more or less since they went abroad" and planned to return to Brooklyn. It mentions that Field and his mother planned to spend the winter in Rome.

9. Importantly, Richardson states that Field met Picasso in his Bateau-Lavoir studio, which would date the meeting to spring 1909. Richardson does not provide the source of his information. See Richardson, *Life of Picasso*, vol. 2, p. 168.

10. For biographical information on the Haviland brothers, see Nicole Maritch-Haviland, *Lalique-Haviland-Burty: Portraits de famille* (Limoges, France: Ardents Editeurs, 2009); and Joséphine Matamoros, *Hommage à Frank Burty Haviland, 1886–1971*, exh. cat. (Céret, France: Musée d'Art Moderne, 2010).

11. Hamilton Easter Field, "At the Brummer Gallery," *Brooklyn Daily Eagle*, December 4, 1921, sec. 3, p. 4. Field also made a passing remark about the intensity of Picasso's eyes in an earlier art column. See Hamilton Easter Field, "At the Daniel Gallery," *Brooklyn Daily Eagle*, March 27, 1921, sec. 3, p. 7. In December 1920, Field launched a new art magazine called *The Arts*, for which he served as both the editor and publisher. In it, he reprinted many of his *Brooklyn Daily Eagle* columns, some with additional illustrations. For reprints of these two texts, see, respectively,

The Editor [Hamilton Easter Field], "Frank Burty," *The Arts* 2, no. 2 (November 1921), pp. 86–89; and The Editor [Hamilton Easter Field], "Comment on the Arts," *The Arts* 1, no. 4 (April 1921), pp. 32–54, esp. 38.

12. For Robert Laurent's life and career, see Peter V. Moak, "Robert Laurent 1890–1970," in *The Robert Laurent Memorial Exhibition, 1972–73*, exh. cat. (Durham, N.H.: University of New Hampshire, 1972), pp. 13–25; and Norman Kent, "Robert Laurent: A Master Carver," *American Artist* 29, no. 5 (May 1965), pp. 42–47, 73–76.

13. Richardson, *Life of Picasso*, vol. 2, p. 171.

14. On Picasso's temporary money issues during the period fall 1909 to spring 1910, see ibid., p. 142.

15. Ibid.

16. Hamilton Easter Field, "Man Ray at the Daniel Gallery," *Brooklyn Daily Eagle*, November 30, 1919, sec. 6, p. 4. Field became the newspaper's art editor in March 1919.

17. Field also remarked on El Greco's influence on Picasso in [Hamilton Easter Field], "Modern French Art at Arden Gallery," *Brooklyn Daily Eagle*, May 18, 1919, sec. 3, p. 11.

18. For Picasso and El Greco, see, for example, Andrea Bayer, "1909: Picasso's Meditation on the Past," in *Cubism: The Leonard A. Lauder Collection*, ed. Emily Braun and Rebecca Rabinow, exh. cat. (New York: The Metropolitan Museum of Art, 2014), pp. 47–58. See also Carmen Giménez and Josef Helfenstein, eds., *Picasso–El Greco*, exh. cat. Kunstmuseum Basel (Berlin: Hatje Cantz, 2022), pp. 114–50.

19. Field, "Man Ray."

20. Elsewhere, however, Field also declared his admiration for Puvis de Chavannes. See Hamilton Easter Field, "Foreword," in *Catalogue of an Exhibition of the Paintings of Hamilton Easter Field*, exh. cat. (New York: Berlin Photographic Company, 1912), pp. 3–10, esp. p. 8. In addition, Field recalled the decorative commissions by Besnard and Puvis de Chavannes in The Editor [Hamilton Easter Field], "Decorations by Paul Burlin," *The Arts* 1, no. 3 (February–March 1921), pp. 30–31.

21. Pablo Picasso, *Sketch of "Saint Geneviève Supplying Paris," by Puvis de Chavannes, in the Pantheon* (1903; Museu Picasso, Barcelona, MPB 110.468). For Picasso's relationship to Puvis de Chavannes, see Richard J. Wattenmaker, *Puvis de Chavannes and the Modern Tradition*, exh. cat. (Toronto: Art Gallery of Ontario, 1975), pp. 162–78. Wattenmaker dates this drawing to about 1901.

22. Hamilton Easter Field, "Brooklyn Art Exhibitions," *Brooklyn Daily Eagle*, March 21, 1920, sec. 6, p. 9.

23. The Corot exhibition was on view from October 1 to November 8, 1909. See "Exposition retrospective de Figures de Corot," in Société du Salon d'Automne, *Catalogue des ouvrages de peinture, sculpture, dessin, gravure, architecture et art décoratif*, exh. cat. (Paris: Société Anonyme de l'Imprimerie Kugelmann, 1909), pp. 215–16. Also, sometime in 1910, Picasso received a small figure painting by Corot from Wilhelm Uhde as a thank-you for painting his portrait, *Portrait of Wilhelm Uhde* (end of 1909–spring 1910; private collection). See Hélène Seckel-Klein with Emmanuelle Chevrière, *Picasso collectionneur* (Paris: Réunion des Musées Nationaux, 1998), pp. 82–84; and Fernande Olivier, *Picasso and His Friends*, trans. Jane Miller (London: Heinemann, 1964), p. 137.

24. Hamilton Easter Field, "Vlaminck at Brummer's," *Brooklyn Daily Eagle*, March 5, 1922, sec. 3, p. C5; reprinted as The Editor [Hamilton Easter Field], "Comment on the Arts," *The Arts* 2, no. 5 (February 1922), pp. 306–28, esp. p. 320.

25. Laurent, "Personal Statement."

26. Richardson, *Life of Picasso*, vol. 2, p. 149.

27. For a discussion of decorative painting during the first decades of the twentieth century, see, for example, Gloria Groom, "Into the Mainstream: Decorative Painting, 1900–30," in *Beyond the Easel: Decorative Painting by Bonnard, Vuillard, Denis, and Roussel, 1890–1930*, ed. Gloria Groom, exh. cat. Art Institute of Chicago; The Metropolitan Museum of Art, New York (Chicago: Art Institute of Chicago; New Haven: Yale University Press, 2001), pp. 143–68.

28. Denis exhibited the works as "L'Histoire de Psyché (5 peintures décoratives, destinée à l'hôtel de M. Y. M. . . . à Moscou)"; see Société du Salon d'Automne, *Catalogue des ouvrages de peinture, sculpture, dessin, gravure, architecture et art décoratif*, exh. cat. (Paris: Librairie Administrative Paul Dupont, 1908), nos. 531–32, pp. 92–93.

29. Ann Temkin and Dorthe Aagesen, eds., *Matisse: The Red Studio*, exh. cat. (New York:

Museum of Modern Art; Copenhagen: SMK—National Gallery of Denmark, 2022), p. 35.

30. Rubin, "Appendix," p. 68.

31. Rubin consulted Daix about the commission while writing his 1989 text. See Rubin, "Appendix," p. 68. Since then, the artistic rivalry between the two men has been presented as the sole factor behind Picasso's acceptance of the commission. See, for example, John Golding, "Catalogue," in Elizabeth Cowling et al., *Matisse Picasso*, exh. cat., Museum of Modern Art, New York; Tate Modern, London; Les Galeries Nationales du Grand Palais, Paris (London: Tate Publishing; Paris: Réunion des Musées Nationaux; New York: Museum of Modern Art, 2002), p. 142; and Stephanie D'Alessandro, "Opportunity and Invention," in Stephanie D'Alessandro and John Elderfield, *Matisse: Radical Invention, 1913–1917*, exh. cat. (Chicago: Art Institute of Chicago; New York: Museum of Modern Art; New Haven: Yale University Press, 2010), pp. 76–86.

32. For Berenson's dealings with Matisse and Piot in regard to the decorative commission for his library, see Hilary Spurling, *Matisse the Master: A Life of Henri Matisse, The Conquest of Colour, 1909–1954* (New York: Alfred A. Knopf, 2005), pp. 38–39, 471–72; and Claudio Pizzorusso, "A Failure: René Piot and the Berensons" and "René Piot" in *The Bernard and Mary Berenson Collection of European Paintings at I Tatti*, eds. Carl Brandon Strehlke and Machtelt Brüggen Israëls (Florence: Villa I Tatti; Milan: Officina Libraria, 2015), pp. 677–89 and 714–21, respectively.

33. Field and his mother are mentioned on several occasions by Mary Berenson in her diaries. Mary Berenson diaries (1891–1909), Florence, Villa I Tatti, The Harvard University Center for Italian Renaissance Studies, Biblioteca Berenson, The Bernard and Mary Berenson Papers (BMBP).

34. Mary Berenson notes in a letter of November 1909 that Field also acquired some of Piot's drawings. See Pizzorusso, "A Failure," pp. 677–78. Field's published recollection doesn't list the date of his visit to Auteuil. However, given that Piot commenced working on the fresco in 1908, and Field didn't return to Europe until 1920—after he published this information—his visit to Gide's house must have taken place during his 1909–10 sojourn in Europe. See Hamilton Easter Field, "French Art at the Metropolitan Museum," *Brooklyn Daily Eagle*, December 21, 1919, sec. 6, p. 7. For Piot's fresco commission for Gide see Rodolphe Rapetti, "René Piot et le renouveau de la fresque à l'aube du XXe siècle," in *René Piot, 1866–1934*, exh. cat. (Paris: Musée d'Orsay; Réunion des Musées Nationaux, 1991), pp. 6–31.

35. Albert Gleizes and Jean Metzinger, *Cubism* (London: T. Fisher Unwin, 1913), p. 19. Originally published in French as *Du "Cubisme"* (Paris: Eugène Figuière et Cie, 1912). The art historian Nancy Troy has argued that Gleizes and Metzinger were reacting to Art Nouveau interiors, in which the integrity of individual paintings was subordinated to "totally harmonious environment." See Nancy Troy, *Modernism and the Decorative Arts in France: Art Nouveau to Le Corbusier* (New Haven: Yale University Press, 1991), p. 95.

36. Gloria Groom, "Coming of Age: Patrons and Projects, 1890–99," in *Beyond the Easel*, pp. 31–57.

37. For the account of Denis's *Psyche* commission, see Anne Baldassari, "Shackled by Psyche," in *The Morozov Collection: Icons of Modern Art*, ed. Anne Baldassari, exh. cat. (Paris: Editions Gallimard; Fondation Louis Vuitton, 2021), pp. 389–93.

38. For recent discussion on Matisse's engagements with various decorative concepts in his easel paintings in the context of his projects for Shchukin, see John Klein, *Matisse and Decoration* (New Haven: Yale University Press, 2018), esp. pp. 53–57. For Matisse's 1911 visit to Moscow, see, for example, Anne Baldassari, "Pink and Black: Shchukin, the Steins, Matisse, Picasso," and "Matisse: The Pink Room," in *Icons of Modern Art: The Shchukin Collection*, ed. Anne Baldassari, exh. cat. (Paris: Editions Gallimard; Fondation Louis Vuitton, 2017), pp. 64–97 and 258–59, respectively.

39. Richardson, *Life of Picasso*, vol. 2, p. 170.

40. The Travelers, *Brooklyn Life*, May 14, 1910, p. 18.

41. Richardson, *Life of Picasso*, vol. 2, p. 172.

42. Gelett Burgess, "The Wild Men of Paris," *Architectural Record* 27, no. 5 (May 1910), pp. 401–14. It is likely that this issue of the magazine was available in Paris soon after its publication. Picasso had a copy by mid-June. See also Cousins, "Documentary Chronology," pp. 365–66.

43. Pablo Picasso to Gertrude Stein, June 14,

1910, Gertrude Stein and Alice B. Toklas Papers, YCAL MSS 76, Box 119, folder 2554, Yale Collection of American Literature, Beinecke Rare Book and Manuscript Library, Yale University.

44. The Travelers, *Brooklyn Life*, May 14, 1910, p. 18.

45. Burty Haviland could have forwarded the letter by post or, given the close proximity of Céret to Cadaqués, delivered it in person. According to a letter to Guillaume Apollinaire, dated August 1, Picasso was expecting a visit from Burty Haviland before long. See Pierre Caizergues and Hélène Seckel, eds., *Picasso/Apollinaire: Correspondance* (Paris: Gallimard; Réunion des Musées Nationaux, 1992), letter no. 45, p. 78.

46. Field briefly studied at Columbia University, New York, and Harvard University, Cambridge, Mass.

47. Field's home and the rest of the Quaker Row properties were acquired by the city of New York in 1946 and demolished in 1947 in connection with the construction of the Brooklyn-Queens Expressway (BQE). See "Roebling House Where Bridge Builder Lived Will Be Demolished," *Brooklyn Daily Eagle*, January 22, 1947, pp. 1, 13. The site of Quaker Row was used for the park areas developed alongside the expressway. This portion of Columbia Heights is now the Fruit Street Sitting Area, which provides access onto the Brooklyn Heights Promenade.

48. The lot size measured 28 feet 9 inches by 150 feet; the house measured 28 feet 9 inches by 60 feet. See Block no. 218, Brooklyn Land Conveyance Collection (1699–1896), Center for Brooklyn History, Brooklyn Public Library. The house was approximately 60 feet deep. See *Atlas of the Borough of Brooklyn, City of New York*, vol. 1 (New York: E. Belcher Hyde, 1903–05), double-page plate no. 4, part of ward 1, sec. 1.

49. Charles Lockwood and Patrick W. Ciccone with Jonathan D. Taylor, *Bricks & Brownstone: The New York Row House* (New York: Rizzoli, 2019), p. 57. The style and plan of the Field residence is closely based on the template for "an ordinary city house, designed to be occupied by one family only," published in R. G. (Robert Griffith) Hatfield, *The American House-Carpenter* (New York: Wiley and Putnam, 1844), pp. 91–96.

50. In the case of 106 Columbia Heights, the house was interlocked with the warehouse at 109 Furman Street (later renumbered to 113 Furman Street). See Block and Lot Index, Register's Office, Kings County, p. 1, sec. 1, block 218, lot 4, street no. 106 Columbia Hgts. 113 Furman St.

51. For the description of Field's Parisian studio, see "A Promising Brooklyn Painter," *Brooklyn Daily Eagle*, March 3, 1901, p. 15.

52. According to a 1905 press account, the house's reception areas continued to reflect the old-fashioned style of Field's parents and grandparents, making the dwelling a well-preserved nineteenth-century time capsule. See "Studio of This Artist Has Superior River Views," *Brooklyn Daily Eagle*, March 19, 1905, p. 19.

53. In addition, just off the studio, there was a "delightful tea and anteroom fitted with divans" trimmed in a "most artistic old blue" as well as a front room facing Columbia Heights, which "has been turned into a non-descript room, more than anything else a music room, also in an old blue." As described in "Studio of This Artist," p. 19.

54. Mary Berenson diary, December 10, 1903, BMBP, 1903–1904 "Trip to America," seq. 111, https://nrs.lib.harvard.edu/urn-3:vit.bb:101386690?n=111.

55. According to Robert Laurent's later recollections, Paul Haviland was a regular visitor to 106 Columbia Heights during the years he lived in New York. Letter from Robert Laurent to John H. Field, November 12, 1969, personal archives of John H. Field.

56. The Week in Society, *Brooklyn Life*, February 17, 1906, p. 21.

57. For Field's interest in Japanese prints and his collection, see William Green, "Hamilton Easter Field (1873–1922)," *Impressions* 8 (Summer 1983), n.p.

58. One of the descriptions of this section of the house comes from Wood Gaylor, an American artist and friend of Robert Laurent, as quoted in Jeffers, "Hamilton Easter Field," p. 34.

59. The tradition of these often large events was established after Field returned from France in 1902. They were initially hosted by Field's mother and regularly featured tours of the house, including Field's studio and his art collection. For later events of this kind, see, for example, "Recital at Field Home," *Brooklyn Daily Eagle*, February 5, 1919, p. 5; "Master School of Music," *Brooklyn Daily Eagle*, February 17, 1919, p. 2.

60. Pablo Picasso to Hamilton Easter Field,

September 1, 1910. This letter is listed with an erroneous date of September 7, 1910, in Rubin, "Appendix," p. 64; Cousins, "Documentary Chronology," p. 369; and Richardson, *Life of Picasso*, vol. 2, p. 165.

61. For Picasso's stay in Cadaqués, see, for example, Pere Vehí, ed., *Cadaqués de Picasso: Centenari de L'estada de Pablo Picasso a Cadaqués, 1910–2010*, exh. cat. (Cadaqués, Spain: Museu de Cadaqués, 2010).

62. Pierre Daix and Joan Rosselet, *Picasso, The Cubist Years, 1907–1916: A Catalogue Raisonné of the Paintings and Related Works*, trans. Dorothy S. Blair (London: Thames and Hudson, 1979), nos. 363 (*Nude Woman*) and 364 (*Woman with a Fan*).

63. Brigitte Baer, *Picasso the Printmaker: Graphics from the Marina Picasso Collection*, ed. Steven A. Nash, exh. cat., Dallas Museum of Art; Brooklyn Museum; Detroit Institute of Arts; Denver Art Museum (Dallas: Dallas Museum of Art, 1983), pp. 35–41.

64. For an in-depth analysis of Picasso's Cubist representations of human anatomy, see Pepe Karmel, "Bodies," in *Picasso and the Invention of Cubism* (New Haven: Yale University Press, 2003), pp. 49–99, esp. pp. 68–87.

65. Emilie Faust, "Technical study no. 12116, Pablo Picasso, *Femme nue debout,"* (unpublished conservation report, Fundación Almine y Bernard Ruiz-Picasso para el Arte, 2022). For a recent discussion of the oil sketch in relation to the painting *Nude Woman* (1910; National Gallery of Art, Washington, D.C.) see Pepe Karmel, "The Human Figure in Picasso's Drawings, 1906–1913," in *Dialogues with Picasso: 2020–2023 Collection* (Málaga, Spain: Fundación Museo Picasso, 2020), pp. 82–119, esp. pp. 104–5.

66. Douglas Cooper, "Picasso's 'Nude Woman' of 1910," *Burlington Magazine* 123, no. 936 (March 1981), pp. 164–65.

67. Henry-Russell Hitchcock, *Painting toward Architecture* (New York: Duell, Sloan and Pearce, 1948), p. 56.

68. Rubin, "Appendix," p. 66.

69. Karmel, *Picasso and the Invention of Cubism*, pp. 141–46.

70. Karmel identified one of these paintings as a work that was initially titled *Monk with Mandolin (Buffalo Bill)* when it was photographed and inventoried by Kahnweiler.

71. Information about the two different ways in which Picasso lengthened the paintings comes from unpublished conservation reports provided by Joanne Snrech, Paintings Conservator, Musée National Picasso-Paris.

72. For the unsubstantiated identification of the work in the photograph as *Man with a Mandolin*, see Annie Cohen-Solal, ed., *Picasso l'étranger*, exh. cat. (Paris: Musée Picasso-Paris; Musée National de l'Histoire de l'Immigration; Fayard, 2021), pp. 96–97.

73. Richardson, *Life of Picasso*, vol. 2, p. 274.

74. For a reproduction of the contract, see "Documents," in Daix and Rosselet, *Picasso: The Cubist Years*, p. 359.

75. Rubin, "Appendix," p. 63; and Cousins, "Documentary Chronology," pp. 375–76.

76. Rubin, "Appendix," p. 66; and *Donation Louise et Michel Leiris: Collection Kahnweiler-Leiris*, exh. cat. (Paris: Musée National d'Art Moderne; Centre Georges Pompidou, 1984), pp. 166–68.

77. Rubin stated that with a magnifying glass he was able "to make out the head, and parts of the bodies, of two figures, as well as fragments of such motifs as a watering can." Rubin, "Appendix," p. 64.

78. The photo in question is *Portrait of Guillaume Apollinaire*, fall 1910 (Picasso Archives, Musée National Picasso-Paris). See Anne Baldassari, *Picasso and Photography: The Dark Mirror*, trans. Deke Dusinberre (Paris: Flammarion; Houston: Museum of Fine Arts, 1997), p. 91, fig. 6.

79. For discussion of this work in relation to Jean Auguste Dominique Ingres's *Grande Odalisque* (1814; Musée du Louvre, Paris) and Edouard Manet's *Olympia* (1863; Musée d'Orsay, Paris), as well as the 1910 photograph of Picasso's studio, see Michael Marrinan, "Picasso as an 'Ingres' Young Cubist," *Burlington Magazine* 119, no. 896, Special Issue Devoted to European Art since 1890 (November 1977), pp. 756, 758–63.

80. Ibid.

81. The title (*Femme couchée sur un divan*) was first published in Christian Zervos's catalogue raisonné. Christian Zervos, *Pablo Picasso*, vol. 2, pt. 2, *Oeuvres de 1912 à 1917* (Paris: Editions "Cahiers d'Art," 1942/1944), no. 727.

82. Robert L. Herbert, *Nature's Workshop: Renoir's Writings on the Decorative Arts* (New Haven: Yale University Press, 2000), esp. pp. 63–87.

83. See Lucy Belloli, "Technical Note," part of

Sabine Rewald's catalogue entry for *Pipe Rack and Still Life on a Table* in *Picasso in The Metropolitan Museum of Art*, ed. Gary Tinterow and Susan Alyson Stein, exh. cat. (New York: The Metropolitan Museum of Art; New Haven: Yale University Press, 2010), p. 158, cat. no. 55.

84. For the two paintings that feature the phrase "& Ocean," see Daix and Rosselet, *Picasso, The Cubist Years,* no. 416 (*Wineglass and Pipe*; summer 1911 [?]) and no. 459 (*Glass of Pernod and Playing Cards*; spring 1912).

85. For the identification of the letters "h e f" as Field's initials, see Rewald, catalogue entry for *Pipe Rack and Still Life on a Table,* in Tinterow and Stein, *Picasso in The Metropolitan Museum of Art*, pp. 156–58, cat. no. 55.

86. Letter from Pablo Picasso to Daniel-Henry Kahnweiler, June 23, 1912, as cited in Cousins, "Documentary Chronology," pp. 396–97.

87. See Daix and Rosselet, *Picasso, The Cubist Years,* no. 418 (*Palette, Brushes, and a Book of Victor Hugo* [*Palette, pinceaux, livre de Victor Hugo*]; summer 1911 [?]).

88. For a recent discussion of Alfred Cortot in relation to the stenciled letters in this painting, see Gabriel Montua, "Nature morte, lettres CORT. *Glissando* de significations," in *Les musiques de Picasso*, ed. Cécile Godefroy, exh. cat. (Paris: Musée de la Musique–Philharmonie de Paris; Gallimard, 2020), pp. 96–99.

89. Cousins, "Documentary Chronology," pp. 387–88.

90. Elizabeth Cowling, "For and against Trompe l'Oeil," in *Cubism and the Trompe l'Oeil Tradition*, ed. Emily Braun and Elizabeth Cowling, exh. cat. (New York: The Metropolitan Museum of Art, 2022), pp. 47–48.

91. For an alternative reading of the relationship between *Still Life on a Piano* and the two Chardin still lifes, see Bernice B. Rose, "Picasso, Braque and Early Film in Cubism," in *Picasso, Braque and Early Film in Cubism*, ed. Bernice B. Rose, exh. cat. (New York: PaceWildenstein, 2007), pp. 34–147, esp. p. 104.

92. The author would like to thank Vérane Tasseau for drawing her attention to this painting.

93. John Richardson with the collaboration of Marilyn McCully, *A Life of Picasso*, vol. 3, *The Triumphant Years, 1917–1932* (London: Pimlico, 2009), p. 74.

94. Charles Brock, "Pablo Picasso: An Intellectual Cocktail," in *Modern Art and America: Alfred Stieglitz and His New York Galleries*, ed. Sarah Greenough, exh. cat. (Washington, D.C.: National Gallery of Art, 2000), pp. 117–25, 497–99, esp. pp. 119–20, nn23–25, p. 498; Herbert J. Seligmann, *Alfred Stieglitz Talking: Notes on Some of His Conversations, 1925–1931* (New Haven: Yale University Library, 1966), pp. 26, 112.

95. Laurent, "A Personal Statement."

96. Alfred Stieglitz to Hamilton Easter Field, October 21, 1911, Alfred Stieglitz/Georgia O'Keeffe Archive, Yale Collection of American Literature, Beinecke Rare Book and Manuscript Library, Yale University, YCAL MSS 85 Box 19, folder 429.

97. Hamilton Easter Field to Alfred Stieglitz, October 25, 1911, Alfred Stieglitz/Georgia O'Keeffe Archive, YCAL MSS 85 Box 19, folder 429, Yale Collection of American Literature, Beinecke Rare Book and Manuscript Library, Yale University.

98. Field, "Foreword," p. 9. For Martin Birnbaum's discussion of his interactions with Field and impression of him, see Martin Birnbaum, *The Last Romantic: The Story of More Than a Half-Century in the World of Art* (New York: Twayne Publishers, 1960), pp. 48–49.

99. [Field], "Modern French Art."

100. Unfortunately, McBride doesn't provide the date of his conversation with Field other than stating that it took place during the early stages of their acquaintance. It is possible that they first met in or after 1913, the year when McBride became an art critic for the New York newspaper *The Sun*. Henry McBride, "Hamilton Easter Field's Career," *The Arts* 3, no. 1 (January 1923), p. 3.

101. Ibid.

102. Lydia Haviland Field died on November 12, 1917. See "Mrs. Aaron Field Dies," *Brooklyn Daily Eagle*, November 12, 1917, p. 2.

103. Field, "Man Ray."

104. Ibid.

105. After 1910, Field, assisted by Laurent, operated a summer art school and colony in Ogunquit, Maine, and an art school (Ardsley School of Modern Art) and a gallery and studios (Ardsley Studios) in Brooklyn Heights (Brooklyn, NY).

106. For an exhibition history of Picasso's work in these and other New York art venues, see Julia May Boddewyn, "Selected Chronology of Exhibitions, Auctions, and Magazine Reproductions, 1910–1957," in Michael FitzGerald, *Picasso and American Art*, exh. cat. Whitney Museum of American Art, New York; San Francisco Museum of Modern Art; Walker Art Center, Minneapolis (New York: Whitney Museum of American Art; New Haven: Yale University Press, 2007), pp. 325–83, esp. pp. 329–30.

107. In his 1919–22 columns on art, Field remarked on seeing works by Picasso at Arden Gallery and The Met, but these were not Cubist.

108. According to *Brooklyn Life*, Field sailed for Naples sometime in May. He was accompanied by Robert Laurent and Laurent's wife. See Summer Plans, *Brooklyn Life*, June 26, 1920, pp. 14-15, esp. p. 15. For his 1920 itinerary, see Hamilton Easter Field's articles in the *Brooklyn Daily Eagle*: "Eagle Art Critic Visits L. Mignon," June 27, 1920, sec. 3, p. 2; "American Academy at Rome Must Have Aid to Expand," July 11, 1920, sec. 3, p. 4; "German Stories of Colored French Troops Propaganda," July 19, 1920, sec. 1, p. 5; "Food Scarce in Munich," July 19, 1920, sec. 1, p. 6; "Eagle Critic Finds Belgium Is Wonder of Europe," July 20, 1920, sec. 1, p. 3; "German Surgeon a Type of Teuton Irreconcilable," July 20, 1920, sec. 1, p. 6; "Belgium Rebuilding Fast; Takes Lead among the Nations," July 26, 1920, sec. 1, p. 4; and "Dusseldorf Still Great Art Center," August 1, 1920, sec. S (Sporting), p. 8.

109. Laurent, "A Personal Statement."

List of Works

1. Douglas Cooper, "Picasso's 'Nude Woman' of 1910," *Burlington Magazine* 123, no. 936 (March 1981), pp. 164–65.

2. Alfred H. Barr Jr., ed., *Picasso: Forty Years of His Art*, exh. cat., Museum of Modern Art, New York; Art Institute of Chicago (New York: Museum of Modern Art, 1939), p. 73, no. 94, black-and-white ill., as *Standing Figure*, 1910 [?], also dated 1911 and 1912.

3. Christian Zervos, *Pablo Picasso*, vol. 2, pt. 1, *Oeuvres de 1906 à 1912* (Paris: Editions "Cahiers d'Art," 1942), no. 233, as *Femme nue*, Cadaqués, summer 1910, 188 × 61 cm, Meric Callery, Paris.

4. Christian Zervos, *Pablo Picasso*, vol. 2, pt. 2, *Oeuvres de 1912 à 1917* (Paris: Editions "Cahiers d'Art," 1942/1944), no. 727, *Femme coucheé sur un divan*, Paris, winter 1910–11, oil on canvas, 30 × 50 cm [erroneous measurement].

5. *Georges Braque, Wassily Kandinsky (1866–1944), Pablo Picasso*, exh. cat. (Zurich: Kunsthaus Zürich, 1946), p. 6, no. 138 (*Komposition*) and no. 137 (*Stilleben, mit Musikinstrumenten*), respectively. They were on loan from the same private collection.

6. See Pepe Karmel, *Picasso and the Invention of Cubism* (New Haven: Yale University Press, 2003), pp. 143–45.

7. Christian Zervos [Mila Gagarine], *Pablo Picasso*, vol. 28, *Supplément aux années 1910–1913* (Paris: Editions "Cahiers d'Art," 1974), no. 57, as *Le guitariste*, 1911, oil on canvas, 155 × 77 cm, collection of the artist.

8. Dominique Bozo, *Picasso: Oeuvres reçues en paiement des droits de succession*, exh. cat., Galeries Nationales du Grand Palais, Paris (Paris: Editions de la Réunion des Musées Nationaux, 1979), no. 48, ill. p. 72.

9. Zervos, *Pablo Picasso*, vol. 2, pt. 1, no. 290, as *Homme à la mandoline*, winter 1911–12, oil on canvas, 158 × 71 cm, collection of the artist.

10. *Hommage à Pablo Picasso* (Paris: Réunion des Musées Nationaux, 1966), cat. no. 76.

11. *Picasso* (Amsterdam: Stedelijk Museum, 1967), no. 28, n.p.

12. Christian Zervos, *Pablo Picasso*, vol. 2, pt. 2, no. 726, as *Pipes, tasse, cafetière, carafon*, Paris, winter 1910–11, oil on canvas, 130 × 50 cm.

13. Christian Zervos, "Peintures de Picasso et de Matisse," *Cahiers d'Art*, nos. 20–21 (1946), p. 428. In addition to *Pipe Rack and Still Life on a Table*, only two other "disappeared" works by Picasso have been recovered to date: *Woman with a Key* (1938; private collection) and *Still Life with Palette* (1938; National Museum of Modern Art, Kyoto); see Christian Zervos, *Pablo Picasso*, vol. 9, *Oeuvres de 1937 à 1939* (Paris: Editions "Cahiers d'Art," 1958), nos. 144 and 235, respectively. For a recent discussion of Zervos's 1946 publication, see Chara Kolokytha, "Matisse, Zervos, and *Cahiers d'art*," in *Matisse in the 1930s*, ed. Colette Taylor-Jones and Jean-Benoit Ormal-Grenon, with the help of Thomas Bari Garnier, trans. Elizabeth G. Heard and John Lee, exh. cat., Philadelphia Museum of Art; Musée de l'Orangerie, Paris; Musée Matisse, Nice (Philadelphia: Philadelphia Museum of Art;

Paris: Réunion des Musées Nationaux-Grand Palais; New Haven: Yale University Press, 2022), pp. 19–30.

14. The black-and-white photograph of the painting published in Zervos's catalogue raisonné and in *Cahiers d'Art* does not show the artist's signature. More research is required to determine the date this photograph was taken. By the time Perls purchased it, the painting was signed. See letter from Klaus G. Perls to Georges Moos, October 6, 1951, Perls Galleries records, 1937–1997, box 15, folder 33, Archives of American Art, Washington, D.C. The approximate dating of the signature was proposed by Christine Pinault of the Picasso Administration and is based on her visual inspection and comparison with the artist's other period signatures. The authors would like to thank Christine Pinault for her expertise.

15. Zervos, *Pablo Picasso*, vol. 2, pt. 2, no. 728, as *Verre à absinthe, bouteille, ventail, pipe, violin, clarinette sur un piano*, Paris, winter 1910–11, oil on canvas, 130 × 50 cm.

16. For the Kunsthaus Zürich exhibition, see note 5. *XXIV Biennale di Venezia*, exh. cat. (Venice: Edizioni Serenissima, 1948), p. 190, no. 3 (*Compozitione*, 1910–11) and no. 6 (*Natura morta con strumenti musicali*, 1912); and Attilio Podestà, "Picasso," in *La XXIV Biennale di Venezia*, exh. cat. (Bergamo: Istituto Italiano d'Arti Grafiche, 1948), pp. 35–40.

17. *Pablo Picasso and Henri Matisse*, exh. cat. (Boston: Museum of Modern Art, 1938), no. 15, n.p.

18. Zervos, *Pablo Picasso*, vol. 2, pt. 2, no. 547, as *Femme à la guitare*, Paris, oil on canvas, 185 x 75 cm, Collection of Walter P. Chrysler Jr.

19. Galerie Pierre advertisement, *Cahiers d'Art*, nos. 8–10 (1937), black-and-white ill., as "Picasso. Peinture. 1911–1918 (1.86 × 0.70)."

20. Valentine Gallery advertisement, *View*, series 4, no. 4 (Dec. 1944), p. 111, black-and-white ill., as "Femme à l'éventail—1912 by Picasso."

21. Zervos, *Pablo Picasso*, vol. 2, pt. 2, no. 944, as *Femme à l'éventail*, Paris, started in 1911, finished in 1918, oil on canvas, dimensions not listed; Galerie Pierre.

22. Henry-Russell Hitchcock, *Painting toward Architecture* (New York: Duell, Sloan and Pearce, 1948), p. 56.

Chronology of the Commission (1909–22)

1. The Travelers, *Brooklyn Life,* February 20, 1909, pp. 18, 20, esp. p. 20; and The Sea Goers, *The Sun*, February 13, 1909, p. 3. They traveled on the North German Lloyd steamship *Barbarossa*, New York–Genoa line, due at Gibraltar on February 22, Naples on February 25, and Genoa on February 26, 1909.

2. Information pertaining to Picasso's whereabouts are drawn from key published chronologies and biographies unless otherwise noted. These include Judith Cousins and Hélène Seckel, "Eléments pour une chronologie de l'histoire des Demoiselles D'Avignon," in *Les Demoiselles d'Avignon*, ed. Hélène Seckel, vol. 2, exh. cat., Musée Picasso, Paris (Paris: Editions de la Réunion des Musées Nationaux, 1988), pp. 547–623; Judith Cousins with the collaboration of Pierre Daix, "Documentary Chronology," in William Rubin, *Picasso and Braque: Pioneering Cubism*, exh. cat. (New York: Museum of Modern Art, 1989), pp. 335–455; "Chronologie documentaire," in *Picasso: Dessins et papiers collés, Céret 1911–1913*, exh. cat. (Céret, France: Musée d'Art Moderne de Céret, 1997), pp. 298–338; John Richardson with the collaboration of Marilyn McCully, *A Life of Picasso*, vol. 2, *The Cubist Rebel, 1907–1916* (New York: Random House, 1996); John Richardson with the collaboration of Marilyn McCully, *A Life of Picasso*, vol. 3, *The Triumphant Years, 1917–1932* (London: Pimlico, 2009); Luise Mahler and Virginie Perdrisot with Rebecca Lowery, "Picasso Sculpture: A Documentary Chronology, 1902–1973," in *Picasso Sculpture*, exh. cat. (New York: Museum of Modern Art, 2015), pp. 31–293.

3. "Florence's Hopes Rest on the Summer Season," *International Herald Tribune*, July 1, 1909, European edition, p. 4.

4. The Travelers, *Brooklyn Life*, October 16, 1909, p. 16. See also "Many Plans Developing for Winter Town Gayety," *The Brooklyn Citizen*, October 17, 1909, p. 7.

5. John Richardson stated that Field visited Picasso "shortly before he moved out of the Bateau-Lavoir" in 1909 but does not provide the source of this information. Richardson, *Life of Picasso*, vol. 2, p. 168.

6. See the postcard from Frank Burty Haviland in *Picasso: Dessins et papiers collés*, p. 308.

7. Hamilton Easter Field, "Man Ray at the Daniel Gallery," *Brooklyn Daily Eagle*, November 30, 1919, sec. 6, p. 4.

8. Robert Laurent, "A Personal Statement," in *The Hamilton Easter Field Art Foundation Collection*, exh. cat. (Ogunquit, Maine: Barn Gallery Associates, 1966), n.p.
9. See note 4.
10. Norman Kent, "Robert Laurent: A Master Carver," *American Artist* 29, no. 5 (May 1965), pp. 42–47, 73–76.
11. The Travelers, *Brooklyn Life*, May 14, 1910, p. 18.
12. Ibid.; and Ship News, *Brooklyn Daily Eagle*, June 21, 1910, p. 5. They traveled on the White Star Line steamship *Adriatic*.
13. Pablo Picasso to Gertrude Stein, n.d., Gertrude and Alice B. Toklas Papers, YCAL MSS 76, Box 119, folder 2554, Series II: Gertrude Stein Correspondence, Picasso, Pablo / 1906–30, n.d. [3 of 8 folders], Yale Collection of American Literature, Beinecke Rare Book and Manuscript Library, Yale University.
14. Hamilton Easter Field to Pablo Picasso, n.d., postmarked Brooklyn, July 12, 1910, Fonds Picasso, series C 1-177 (correspondance générale), classeur 47, Picasso Archives, Musée National Picasso-Paris. Translated from the French by John Goodman.
15. Pablo Picasso to Hamilton Easter Field, September 1, 1910, private collection. Translated from the French by John Goodman.
16. Herbert J. Seligmann, *Alfred Stieglitz Talking: Notes on Some of His Conversations, 1925–1931* (New Haven: Yale University Library, 1966), pp. 26, 112.
17. William Rubin, "Picasso and Braque: An Introduction," in William Rubin, *Picasso and Braque: Pioneeering Cubism*, exh. cat. (New York: Museum of Modern Art, 1989), pp. 15–62, esp p. 54n3. See also in Rubin, *Picasso and Braque*: Rubin, "Appendix," pp. 64, 69n6; and Cousins, "Documentary Chronology," pp. 375–76.
18. Alfred Stieglitz to Hamilton Easter Field, October 21, 1911, Alfred Stieglitz/Georgia O'Keeffe Archive, YCAL MSS 85, Box 19, folder 429, Series I: Alfred Stieglitz Correspondence, Field, Hamilton Easter 1911–21, Yale Collection of American Literature, Beinecke Rare Book and Manuscript Library, Yale University.
19. For a reproduction of the letter, see *Donation Louise et Michel Leiris: Collection Kahnweiler-Leiris*, exh. cat. (Paris: Musée National d'Art Moderne; Centre Georges Pompidou, 1984), pp. 166–67.
20. For a reproduction of the contract, see "Documents," in Pierre Daix and Joan Rosselet, *Le cubisme de Picasso: Catalogue raisonné de l'oeuvre peint, 1907–1916* (Neuchâtel, Switzerland: Editions Ides et Calendes, 1979), p. 359.
21. "Mrs. Aaron Field Dies," *Brooklyn Daily Eagle*, November 12, 1917, p. 2.
22. Henry McBride, "Hamilton Easter Field's Career," *The Arts* 3, no. 1 (January 1923), p. 3.
23. Field, "Man Ray."
24. See, for example, "Hamilton E. Field, Well Known Artist, Eagle Critic, Dies," *Brooklyn Daily Eagle*, April 10, 1922, sec. 1, p. 3; and "Hamilton E. Field, Artist, Left Bulk of Estate to Friend," *Brooklyn Daily Eagle*, April 22, 1922, sec. 1, p. 2.
25. *Selections from the Library of the Late Hamilton Easter Field of Brooklyn, N.Y.*, sale cat. (New York: The American Art Galleries, December 5, 1922).
26. "Roebling House Where Bridge Builder Lived Will Be Demolished," *Brooklyn Daily Eagle*, January 22, 1947, pp. 1, 13.

SELECTED BIBLIOGRAPHY

New York newspapers and magazines played an essential role in establishing a fuller picture of Hamilton Easter Field's life and travels, including his interactions with Pablo Picasso. Because of the importance of these sources, they appear separately, with entries in chronological order.

NEWSPAPER AND MAGAZINE SOURCES

***The Arts*, Brooklyn, New York, vols. 1–2; subsequently New York, New York**

The Editor [Hamilton Easter Field]. "Decorations by Paul Burlin," *The Arts* 1, no. 3 (February–March 1921), pp. 30–31.

———. "Comment on the Arts," *The Arts* 1, no. 4 (April 1921), pp. 32–54.

———. "Frank Burty," *The Arts* 2, no. 2 (November 1921), pp. 86–89.

———. "Comment on the Arts," *The Arts* 2, no. 5 (February 1922), pp. 306–28.

McBride, Henry. "Hamilton Easter Field's Career." *The Arts* 3, no. 1 (January 1923), p. 3.

***The Brooklyn Citizen*, Brooklyn, New York**

"Many Plans Developing for Winter Town Gayety," October 17, 1909, p. 7.

***The Brooklyn Daily Eagle*, Brooklyn, New York**

"A Promising Brooklyn Painter," March 3, 1901, p. 15.

"Studio of This Artist Has Superior River Views," March 19, 1905, p. 19.

Ship News, June 21, 1910, p. 5.

"Mrs. Aaron Field Dies," November 12, 1917, p. 2.

"Recital at Field Home," February 5, 1919, p. 5.

"Master School of Music," February 17, 1919, p. 2.

[Field, Hamilton Easter]. "Modern French Art at Arden Gallery," May 18, 1919, sec. 3, p. 11.

Field, Hamilton Easter. "Courbet Centenary Exhibition At the Metropolitan Museum," April 13, 1919, sec. 3, p. 10.

———. "Man Ray at the Daniel Gallery," November 30, 1919, sec. 6, p. 4.

———. "French Art at the Metropolitan Museum," December 21, 1919, sec. 6, p. 7.

———. "Brooklyn Art Exhibitions," March 21, 1920, sec. 6, p. 9.

———. "Eagle Art Critic Visits L. Mignon," June 27, 1920, sec. 3, p. 2.

———. "American Academy at Rome Must Have Aid to Expand," July 11, 1920, sec. 3, p. 4.

———. "German Stories of Colored French Troops Propaganda," July 19, 1920, sec. 1, p. 5.

———. "Food Scarce in Munich," July 19, 1920, sec. 1, p. 6.

———. "Eagle Critic Finds Belgium Is Wonder of Europe," July 20, 1920, sec. 1, p. 3.

———. "German Surgeon a Type of Teuton Irreconcilable," July 20, 1920, sec. 1, p. 6.

———. "Belgium Rebuilding Fast; Takes Lead among the Nations," July 26, 1920, sec. 1, p. 4.

———. "Dusseldorf Still Great Art Center," August 1, 1920, sec. S (Sporting), p. 8.

———. "Egyptian Antiquities at the Metropolitan Museum," December 19, 1920, sec. 3, p. 6.

———. "At the Daniel Gallery," March 27, 1921, sec. 3, p. 7.

———. "At the Brummer Gallery," December 4, 1921, sec. 3, p. 4.

———. "Vlaminck at Brummer's," March 5, 1922, sec. 3, p. C5.

"Hamilton E. Field, Well Known Artist, Eagle Critic, Dies," April 10, 1922, sec. 1, p. 3.

"Hamilton E. Field, Artist, Left Bulk of Estate to Friend," April 22, 1922, sec. 1, p. 2.

"Roebling House Where Bridge Builder Lived Will Be Demolished," January 22, 1947, pp. 1, 13.

***Brooklyn Life: The Illustrated Home Weekly for Brooklyn and Long Island*, Brooklyn, New York**
The Week in Society, February 17, 1906, p. 21.

The Travelers, February 20, 1909, pp. 18, 20.

The Travelers, October 16, 1909, p. 16.

The Travelers, May 14, 1910, p. 18.

J. W. "Exhibition of the Work of Mr. Hamilton Easter Field and Mr. Robert Laurent," March 27, 1915, p. 10.

"Mrs. Aaron Field," March 25, 1916, p. 124.

Summer Plans, June 26, 1920, pp. 14–15.

***International Herald Tribune*, New York, New York**
"Florence's Hopes Rest on the Summer Season," July 1, 1909, European edition, p. 4.

***The International Studio: An Illustrated Magazine of Fine and Applied Art*, New York, New York**
Nelson, W. H. de B. "Sincerity in Art: Hamilton Easter Field." *The International Studio* 59, no. 233 (July 1916), pp. 22–25.

***The Sun*, New York, New York**
The Sea Goers, February 13, 1909, p. 3.

OTHER PUBLISHED SOURCES

Baer, Brigitte. *Picasso the Printmaker: Graphics from the Marina Picasso Collection*. Edited by Steven A. Nash. Exh. cat. Dallas Museum of Art; Brooklyn Museum; Detroit Institute of Arts; Denver Art Museum; 1983–84. Dallas: Dallas Museum of Art, 1983.

Baldassari, Anne, ed. *Icons of Modern Art: The Shchukin Collection*. Exh. cat. Paris: Editions Gallimard; Fondation Louis Vuitton, 2017. [French ed., *Icônes de l'art moderne: La collection Chtchoukine.*]

———, ed. *The Morozov Collection: Icons of Modern Art*. Exh. cat. Paris: Editions Gallimard, Fondation Louis Vuitton, 2021. [French ed., *La collection Morozov: Icônes de l'art moderne*.]

———. *Picasso and Photography: The Dark Mirror*. Translated by Deke Dusinberre. Paris: Flammarion; Houston: Museum of Fine Arts, 1997.

Barr, Alfred H., Jr., ed. *Picasso: Forty Years of His Art*. Exh. cat. Museum of Modern Art, New York; Art Institute of Chicago; 1939–40. New York: Museum of Modern Art, 1939.

Berenson, Mary. Mary Berenson diaries. Florence, Villa I Tatti, The Harvard University Center for Italian Renaissance Studies, Biblioteca Berenson, The Bernard and Mary Berenson Papers (BMBP). Digitized at https://hollisarchives.lib.harvard.edu/repositories/10/archival_objects/2166969.

Birnbaum, Martin. *The Last Romantic: The Story of More Than a Half-Century in the World of Art.* New York: Twayne Publishers, 1960.

Bolger, Doreen. "Hamilton Easter Field and His Contribution to American Modernism." *American Art Journal* (Kennedy Galleries) 20, no. 2 (1988), pp. 78–107.

———. "Hamilton Easter Field and the Rise of Modern Art in America." Master's thesis, University of Delaware, 1973.

Bozo, Dominique. *Picasso: Oeuvres reçues en paiement des droits de succession.* Exh. cat. Galeries Nationale du Grand Palais, Paris; 1979–80. Paris: Editions de la Réunion des Musées Nationaux, 1979.

Braun, Emily, and Elizabeth Cowling, eds. *Cubism and the Trompe l'Oeil Tradition.* Exh. cat. New York: The Metropolitan Museum of Art, 2022.

Braun, Emily, and Rebecca Rabinow, eds. *Cubism: The Leonard A. Lauder Collection*. Exh. cat. New York: The Metropolitan Museum of Art, 2014.

Burgess, Gelett. "The Wild Men of Paris." *Architectural Record* 27, no. 5 (May 1910), pp. 401–14.

Burke, Colin B. *Information and Intrigue: From Index Cards to Dewey Decimals to Alger Hiss*. Cambridge, Mass.: MIT Press, 2014.

Caizergues, Pierre, and Hélène Seckel, eds. *Picasso/Apollinaire: Correspondance*. Paris: Gallimard; Réunion des Musées Nationaux, 1992.

Catalogue of an Exhibition of the Paintings of Hamilton Easter Field. Exh. cat. New York: Berlin Photographic Company, 1912.

Cohen-Solal, Annie, ed. *Picasso l'étranger*. Exh. cat. Paris: Musée Picasso-Paris; Musée National de l'Histoire de l'Immigration; Fayard, 2021.

Cooper, Douglas. "Picasso's 'Nude Woman' of 1910." *Burlington Magazine* 123, no. 936 (March 1981), pp. 164–65.

Cowling, Elizabeth, Anne Baldassari, John Elderfield, John Golding, Isabelle Monod-Fontaine, and Kirk Varnedoe. *Matisse Picasso*. Exh. cat. Museum of Modern Art, New York; Tate Modern, London; Les Galeries Nationale du Grand Palais, Paris; 2002–3. London: Tate Publishing; Paris: Réunion des Musées Nationaux; New York: Museum of Modern Art, 2002.

Daix, Pierre, and Joan Rosselet. *Picasso, The Cubist Years, 1907–1916: A Catalogue Raisonné of the Paintings and Related Works*. Translated by Dorothy S. Blair. London: Thames and Hudson, 1979. [French ed., *Le cubisme de Picasso: Catalogue raisonné de l'oeuvre peint, 1907–1916*. Neuchâtel, Switzerland: Editions Ides et Calendes, 1979.]

D'Alessandro, Stephanie, and John Elderfield. *Matisse: Radical Invention, 1913–1917*. Exh. cat. Chicago: Art Institute of Chicago; New York: Museum of Modern Art; New Haven: Yale University Press, 2010.

Dialogues with Picasso: 2020–2023 Collection. Málaga, Spain: Fundación Museo Picasso, 2020.

Donation Louise et Michel Leiris: Collection Kahnweiler-Leiris. Exh. cat. Paris: Musée National d'Art Moderne; Centre Georges Pompidou, 1984.

FitzGerald, Michael. *Picasso and American Art*. With a chronology by Julia May Boddewyn. Exh. cat. Whitney Museum of American Art, New York; San Francisco Museum of Modern Art; Walker Art Center, Minneapolis; 2006–7. New York: Whitney Museum of American Art; New Haven: Yale University Press, 2007.

Georges Braque, Wassily Kandinsky (1866–1944), Pablo Picasso. Exh. cat. Zurich: Kunsthaus Zürich, 1946.

Giménez, Carmen, and Josef Helfenstein, eds. *Picasso–El Greco*. Exh. cat. Kunstmuseum Basel. Berlin: Hatje Cantz, 2022.

Gleizes, Albert, and Jean Metzinger. *Cubism*. London: T. Fisher Unwin, 1913. [French ed., *Du "Cubisme*." Paris: Eugène Figuière et Cie, 1912.]

Godefroy, Cécile, ed. *Les musiques de Picasso*. Exh. cat. Paris: Musée de la Musique–Philharmonie de Paris; Gallimard, 2020.

Green, William. "Hamilton Easter Field (1873–1922)." *Impressions* 8 (summer 1983), n.p.

Greenough, Sarah, ed. *Modern Art and America: Alfred Stieglitz and His New York Galleries*. Exh. cat. Washington, D.C.: National Gallery of Art, 2000.

Groom, Gloria, ed. *Beyond the Easel: Decorative Painting by Bonnard, Vuillard, Denis, and Roussel, 1890–1930*. Exh. cat. Art Institute of Chicago; The Metropolitan Museum of Art, New York. Chicago: Art Institute of Chicago; New Haven: Yale University Press, 2001.

The Hamilton Easter Field Art Foundation Collection. Exh. cat. Ogunquit, Maine: Barn Gallery Associates, 1966.

Hatfield, R. G. (Robert Griffith). *The American House-Carpenter: A Treatise upon Architecture, Cornices and Mouldings, Framing, Doors, Windows, and Stairs. Together with the Most*

Important Principles of Practical Geometry. New York: Wiley and Putnam, 1844.

Herbert, Robert L. *Nature's Workshop: Renoir's Writings on the Decorative Arts*. New Haven: Yale University Press, 2000.

Hitchcock, Henry-Russell. *Painting toward Architecture*. New York: Duell, Sloan and Pearce, 1948.

Hommage à Pablo Picasso. Paris: Réunion des Musées Nationaux, 1966.

Jeffers, Wendy. "Hamilton Easter Field: The Benefactor from Brooklyn." *Archives of American Art Journal* 50, no. 1/2 (Spring 2011), pp. 26–37.

Karmel, Pepe. *Picasso and the Invention of Cubism*. New Haven: Yale University Press, 2003.

Kent, Norman. "Robert Laurent: A Master Carver." *American Artist* 29, no. 5 (May 1965), pp. 42–47, 73–76.

Klein, John. *Matisse and Decoration*. New Haven: Yale University Press, 2018.

Kolokytha, Chara. "Matisse, Zervos, and *Cahiers d'art*." In *Matisse in the 1930s*, edited by Collette Taylor-Jones and Jean-Benoit Ormal-Grenon, with the help of Thomas Bari Garnier, translated by Elizabeth G. Heard and John Lee, pp. 19–30. Exh. cat., Philadelphia Museum of Art; Musée de l'Orangerie, Paris; Musée Matisse, Nice; 2022–23. Philadelphia: Philadelphia Museum of Art; Paris: Réunion des Musées Nationaux-Grand Palais; New Haven: Yale University Press, 2022.

Lockwood, Charles, and Patrick W. Ciccone with Jonathan D. Taylor. *Bricks & Brownstone: The New York Row House*. New York: Rizzoli, 2019.

Maritch-Haviland, Nicole. *Lalique-Haviland-Burty: Portraits de famille*. Limoges, France: Ardents Editeurs, 2009.

Marrinan, Michael. "Picasso as an 'Ingres' Young Cubist." *Burlington Magazine* 119, no. 896, Special Issue Devoted to European Art since 1890 (November 1977), pp. 756, 758–63.

Matamoros, Joséphine. *Hommage à Frank Burty Haviland, 1886–1971*. Exh. cat. Céret, France: Musée d'Art Moderne, 2010.

Olivier, Fernande. *Picasso and His Friends*. Translated by Jane Miller. London: Heinemann, 1964.

Pablo Picasso and Henri Matisse. Exh. cat. Boston: Museum of Modern Art, 1938.

Picasso. Exh. cat. Amsterdam: Stedelijk Museum, 1967, no. 28, n.p.

Picasso: Dessins et papiers collés, Céret 1911–1913. Exh. cat. Céret, France: Musée d'Art Moderne de Céret, 1997.

Picasso Sculpture. Exh. cat. New York: Museum of Modern Art, 2015.

René Piot, 1866–1934. Exh. cat. Paris: Musée d'Orsay; Paris: Réunion des Musées Nationaux, 1991.

Richardson, John, with the collaboration of Marilyn McCully. *A Life of Picasso*. Vol. 2, *The Cubist Rebel, 1907–1916*. New York: Random House, 1996. [Reprinted as *A Life of Picasso: The Cubist Rebel, 1907–1916*. New York: Alfred A. Knopf, 2007.]

———. *A Life of Picasso*. Vol. 3, *The Triumphant Years, 1917–1932*. London: Pimlico, 2009.

The Robert Laurent Memorial Exhibition, 1972–73. Exh. cat. Durham, N.H.: University of New Hampshire, 1972.

Rose, Bernice B., ed. *Picasso, Braque and Early Film in Cubism*. Exh. cat. New York: PaceWildenstein, 2007.

Rubin, William. *Picasso and Braque: Pioneering Cubism*. Exh. cat. New York: Museum of Modern Art, 1989. [French ed., *Picasso et Braque: L'Invention du Cubisme*. Paris: Flammarion, 1990. German ed., *Picasso und Braque: Die Geburt des Kubismus*. Munich: Prestel, 1990. Spanish ed., *Picasso y*

Braque: La invención del Cubismo. Barcelona: Ediciones Polígrafa, 1991.]

Ryan, Hugh. *When Brooklyn Was Queer*. New York: St. Martin's Press, 2019.

Seckel, Hélène, ed. *Les Demoiselles d'Avignon*, vol. 2. Exh. cat. Musée Picasso, Paris. Paris: Réunion des Musées Nationaux, 1988.

Seckel-Klein, Hélène, with Emmanuelle Chevrière. *Picasso collectionneur*. Paris: Réunion des Musées Nationaux, 1998.

Selections from the Library of the Late Hamilton Easter Field of Brooklyn, N.Y. Sale cat. The American Art Galleries, New York, December 5, 1922.

Seligmann, Herbert J. *Alfred Stieglitz Talking: Notes on Some of His Conversations, 1925–1931.* New Haven: Yale University Library, 1966.

Société du Salon d'Automne. *Catalogue des ouvrages de peinture, sculpture, dessin, gravure, architecture et art décoratif*. Exh. cat. Paris: Librairie Administrative Paul Dupont, 1908.

———. *Catalogue des ouvrages de peinture, sculpture, dessin, gravure, architecture et art décoratif*. Exh. cat. Paris: Société Anonyme de l'Imprimerie Kugelmann, 1909.

Spurling, Hilary. *Matisse the Master: A Life of Henri Matisse, The Conquest of Colour, 1909–1954*. New York: Alfred A. Knopf, 2005.

Strehlke, Carl Brandon, and Machtelt Brüggen Israëls, eds. *The Bernard and Mary Berenson Collection of European Paintings at I Tatti*. Florence: Villa I Tatti; Milan: Officina Libraria, 2015.

Temkin, Ann, and Dorthe Aagesen, eds. *Matisse: The Red Studio*. Exh. cat.; 2022–23. New York: Museum of Modern Art; Copenhagen: SMK—National Gallery of Denmark, 2022.

Tinterow, Gary, and Susan Alyson Stein, eds. *Picasso in The Metropolitan Museum of Art*. Exh. cat. New York: The Metropolitan Museum of Art; New Haven: Yale University Press, 2010.

Troy, Nancy. *Modernism and the Decorative Arts in France: Art Nouveau to Le Corbusier*. New Haven: Yale University Press, 1991.

La XXIV Biennale di Venezia. Exh. cat. Bergamo: Istituto Italiano d'Arti Grafiche, 1948.

XXIV Biennale di Venezia. Exh. cat. Venice: Edizioni Serenissima, 1948.

Vehí, Pere, ed. *Cadaqués de Picasso: Centenari de L'Estada de Pablo Picasso a Cadaqués, 1910–2010*. Exh. cat. Cadaqués, Spain: Museu de Cadaqués, 2010.

Wattenmaker, Richard J. *Puvis de Chavannes and the Modern Tradition*. Exh. cat. Toronto: Art Gallery of Ontario, 1975.

Zervos, Christian [Mila Gagarine]. *Pablo Picasso.* Vol. 28, *Supplément aux années 1910–1913.* Paris: Editions "Cahiers d'Art," 1974.

Zervos, Christian. *Pablo Picasso*. Vol. 2, pt. 1, *Oeuvres de 1906 à 1912*. Paris: Editions "Cahiers d'Art," 1942.

———. *Pablo Picasso*. Vol. 2, pt. 2, *Oeuvres de 1912 à 1917*. Paris: Editions "Cahiers d'Art," 1942/1944.

———. *Pablo Picasso*. Vol. 9, *Oeuvres de 1937 à 1939*. Paris: Editions "Cahiers d'Art," 1958.

———. "Peintures de Picasso et de Matisse." *Cahiers d'Art*, nos. 20–21 (1946), p. 248.

Page numbers in *italics* refer to illustrations.

This catalogue is published in conjunction with *Picasso: A Cubist Commission in Brooklyn*, on view at The Metropolitan Museum of Art, New York, from September 14, 2023, through January 14, 2024. It is the second in a series of focused research exhibitions under the auspices of the Leonard A. Lauder Research Center for Modern Art.

The exhibition and this publication are made possible by the Leonard A. Lauder Research Center for Modern Art.

This exhibition is a participant in the international Celebration Picasso 1973–2023, which marks the fiftieth anniversary of the artist's death.

Picasso
Celebration
— 1973.2023

Published by The Metropolitan Museum of Art, New York
Mark Polizzotti, Publisher and Editor in Chief
Peter Antony, Associate Publisher for Production
Michael Sittenfeld, Associate Publisher for Editorial

Edited by Kayla Elam
Production by Peter Antony
Designed by Roy Brooks, Fold Four, Inc.
Bibliographic editing by Eleanor Hughes
Image acquisitions and permissions by Elizabeth De Mase
Translations from French by John Goodman

Photographs of works in The Met collection are by the Imaging Department, The Metropolitan Museum of Art, unless otherwise noted.

Pablo Picasso's art, writings, personal photographs, and archival material are © 2023 Estate of Pablo Picasso / Artists Rights Society (ARS), New York. Additional photography credits: front cover: © RMN-Grand Palais / Art Resource, NY; back cover: © RMN-Grand Palais / Art Resource, NY, photo by Mathieu Rabeau; p. 2, pls. 8, 9: © RMN-Grand Palais / Art Resource, NY, photo by Adrien Didierjean; p. 4, fig. 28, pls. 4, 7, 10, 12: Image © Metropolitan Museum of Art; p. 10, pl. 1: Courtesy National Gallery of Art, Washington; fig. 1: © 2023 Artists Rights Society (ARS), New York, Photo © RMN-Grand Palais / Art Resource, NY, photo by Alexis Brandt; fig. 2: © RMN-Grand Palais / Art Resource, NY. "Marguerite" by Henri Matisse (RF1973-77) © 2023 Succession H. Matisse / Artists Rights Society (ARS), New York; fig. 3: © 2023 Succession H. Matisse / Artists Rights Society (ARS), New York, Photo courtesy Archives Henri Matisse; fig. 4: From *Apollon*, vol. 3, pt. 1, nos. 3–4, S. K. Makovskiĭ, Petrograd, Saint Petersburg, 1909–1917. Image © Metropolitan Museum of Art, photo by Teri Aderman; figs. 5, 6, 18, 24, pp. 90–91: © RMN-Grand Palais / Art Resource, NY, photo by Mathieu Rabeau; fig. 7: The New York Public Library; fig. 8: From the Collection of Bob Stonehill; fig. 9: Photo © New-York Historical Society; fig. 11: MC 4, Roebling Collection, Institute Archives and Special Collections, Rensselaer Polytechnic Institute, Troy, NY; fig. 12: From *The International Studio: An Illustrated Monthly Magazine of Fine & Applied Art*, vol. LIX, no. 233, John Lane, New York, 1897–1931, p. XII. Image © Metropolitan Museum of Art, photo by Teri Aderman; fig. 13: © 2023 Artists Rights Society (ARS), New York, Photo © RMN-Grand Palais / Art Resource, NY, photo by René-Gabriel Ojeda; fig. 14: Brooklyn Public Library, Center for Brooklyn History; fig. 16: Photo by François Fernandez; figs. 17, 20, 21, 29: © RMN-Grand Palais / Art Resource, NY; fig. 19: © Archives Olga Ruiz-Picasso, Fundación Almine y Bernard Ruiz-Picasso para el Arte, Madrid; fig. 22: © RMN-Grand Palais / Art Resource, NY, photo by by Madeleine Coursaget; fig. 23: From *Picasso, Ingres*, Réunion des Musées Nationaux, Paris, 2004, p. 99, cat. 27. Image © Metropolitan Museum of Art, photo by Teri Aderman; fig. 25: © RMN-Grand Palais / Art Resource, NY, photo by Stéphane Maréchalle; fig. 26: BF918, The Barnes Foundation, Philadelphia; fig. 27: BF919, The Barnes Foundation, Philadelphia; figs. 30, 31: © 2023 Artists Rights Society (ARS), New York / ADAGP, Paris, The Solomon R. Guggenheim Foundation / Art Resource, NY; figs. 32, 33: Erich Lessing / Art Resource, NY; fig. 33: Photo © 2023 Museum of Fine Arts, Boston; p. 57, pl. 11: Photo by Peter Schälchli; pl. 2: Courtesy Pace Gallery; pl. 3: Photo by Michael Bodycomb; pl. 5: bpk Bildagentur / Staatsgalerie Stuttgart, Graphische Sammlung / Art Resource, NY; pl. 6: © Fundación Almine y Bernard Ruiz-Picasso para el Arte, Madrid, photo by Marc Domage; pl. 13: bpk / Nationalgalerie, SMB, Museum Berggruen / Jens Ziehe; pl. 14: Ugo Bozzi Editore Srl - Roma; pl. 15: From *The Tremaine Collection: 20th Century Masters: The Spirit of Modernism*, Wadsworth Atheneum, Hartford, Connecticut, 1984, p. 35. Image © Metropolitan Museum of Art, photo by Teri Aderman; p. 89: Gertrude Stein and Alice B. Toklas Papers, Yale Collection of American Literature, Beinecke Rare Book and Manuscript Library; p. 92: Courtesy of Swann Auction Galleries; p. 94: Alfred Stieglitz / Georgia O'Keeffe Archive. Yale Collection of American Literature, Beinecke Rare Book and Manuscript Library

Typeset in News Gothic BT and Trade Gothic LT Pro
Printed on 170 gsm Magno Volume
Color separations, printing, and binding by Trifolio S.r.l., Verona, Italy

Cover illustrations: front, Pablo Picasso in his boulevard Raspail studio, 1913 (fig. 21); back, letter from Hamilton Easter Field to Pablo Picasso, postmarked July 12, 1910 (p. 90, detail). Frontispiece details: p. 2: Pablo Picasso, *Man with a Guitar*, summer/fall 1911, reworked in 1913 (pl. 8); p. 4: Pablo Picasso, *Pipe Rack and Still Life on a Table*, summer 1911 (pl. 12); p. 10: Pablo Picasso, *Nude Woman*, summer or fall 1910 (pl. 1); p. 57: Pablo Picasso, *Reclining Woman on a Sofa*, fall 1910 (pl. 11)

First printing

The Metropolitan Museum of Art
1000 Fifth Avenue
New York, New York 10028
metmuseum.org

Distributed by
Yale University Press, New Haven and London
yalebooks.com/art
yalebooks.co.uk

Cataloguing-in-Publication Data is available from the Library of Congress.
ISBN 978-1-58839-768-3